THE REAL
DICKENS LAND

ROCHESTER CASTLE, FROM THE BRIDGE.

Phot.^d in America.   J.C.Armytage.

CHARLES DICKENS.

ÆT. 56.

CHARLES DICKENS'S RULE OF LIFE

> *" Whatever I have tried to do in life, I have tried with all my heart to do well. What I have devoted myself to, I have devoted myself to completely.   Never to put one hand to anything on which I could not throw my whole self, and never to affect depreciation of my work, whatever it was, I find now to have been one of my golden rules."*—David Copperfield.

GREAT HALL OF THE MIDDLE TEMPLE.

Where Charles Dickens was entered as a student.

THE REAL
DICKENS LAND

WITH AN OUTLINE OF DICKENS'S LIFE

BY

H. SNOWDEN WARD

AND

CATHARINE WEED BARNES WARD

Authors of "Shakespeare's Town and Times"

LONDON

CHAPMAN & HALL, LIMITED

1904

CONTENTS ❧ ❧

❧ ❧ INTRODUCTION

In reading and re-reading the works of Dickens, with the light thrown upon them by Forster's *Life*, and in tracing for ourselves the footsteps of the great author and of some of his characters, we have been forced to the conclusion that Dickens was notable for his sentiment of locality. His understanding of the human character is apparent to every good reader of his works ; but his intimate knowledge of the "character" of places, and of the important effect of place upon the human being, is not so apparent, because the reader has not the necessary knowledge of the places. This we have tried to supply. We hope that we have been able to show, and not merely to say, that Dickens felt and realised the influence of trees and fields ; of smoke-grimed bricks and broken window-panes ; for does he not place Jerry Cruncher in Hanging Sword Alley, Fagin near Field Lane, Gabriel Varden near St. John's Gate, Clerkenwell, and Little Nell in the fields and lanes of the English Midlands ?

In our identifications we have gone *first* to Dickens ; later to some of his excellent commentators—Forster, Fitzgerald, Kitton, Hughes, Rimmer, Allbut, Langton, Hammond Hall, Frost, and others whose writings are accessible ; and to a very great number of private correspondents whose love of Dickens and knowledge of a certain district have enabled them to give material help. In selecting a house, a street, or in some cases even a town for illustration, we have not necessarily argued that that particular place was definitely in Dickens's mind at the time of writing. In most cases his descriptions are so clear that there can be no hesitation. In other cases, left purposely more vague, our care has been, firstly, that the place was known to Dickens ; secondly, that it is in keeping with such description as is given ; thirdly, that it is at least as likely as any other place ; and fourthly, that it still recalls the spirit of the scene. In such a case as the King's Head, Chigwell, *versus* the Maypole, Chigwell Green, we take the evidence in Forster's *Life* as to the place Dickens actually visited ; in such a case as the Dombey house, we frankly state the item of the description with which it fails to agree ; and in dealing with Canterbury, where authorities absolutely differ, we leave the scenes as unidentified, although in the London district around Golden Square (*Nickleby*), where streets are but vaguely mentioned, we have not hesitated to accept a typical street and a typical house therein.

To deal with the whole of Dickens Land in one volume of reasonable size is impossible, hence we have narrowed the field by confining ourselves entirely to England, essentially *the* land of Dickens, though much interest might have been added by including some of the Continental and American scenes.

Our book probably contains errors. We know that it is far from complete, and that in selecting the subjects for illustration we have left in our negative boxes a still greater number of perhaps equally interesting subjects. Readers' corrections and suggestions will be very greatly valued.

When we began this work we began to compile a list of those to whom we were indebted for assistance, but it has grown so long as to become unwieldy, wherefore we are obliged to express our thanks as we do, most sincerely, in this general paragraph.

THE HIGH STREET, ROCHESTER.

"Most of us come from Dullborough who come from a country town. . . . I had entertained the impression that the High Street was at least as wide as Regent Street, London. I found it little better than a lane. A clock which I supposed to be the finest in the world . . . . turned out to be as inexpressive, moon-faced, and weak a clock as ever I saw."—*The Uncommercial Traveller.*

ROCHESTER CASTLE.

"Centuries have so defaced the apertures in its walls that the ruin looks as if the rooks and daws had pecked its eyes out."—*Seven Poor Travellers.*

CHAPTER I

Dickens's Childhood

PORTSMOUTH ; LONDON ; CHATHAM ; AND FIRST GLIMPSES OF GADSHILL ; 1812–1823

CHARLES DICKENS was the son of John Dickens, a clerk in the pay-office of the Royal Navy, and a man whose character and circumstances probably had more to do with his son's success than has been generally admitted. The one advantage possessed by Charles as compared with his father was his slightly greater appreciation of the value of money ; but apart from this his character seems to have been simply a stronger and a somewhat more carefully controlled version of his father's. John Dickens suffered for his very virtues, since his careless generosity was largely responsible for landing him in a debtors' prison and making him a bankrupt. Besides this generosity, and the hospitality which were so strongly

THE FALSTAFF, GADSHILL.

marked in his son's character, John Dickens had great versatility and power of application, a strong sense of humour, quick observa-

ST. MARY-IN-THE-STRAND.
John Dickens married Elizabeth Barrow, June 13, 1809.

tion, wide sympathies, and a fund of anecdote. Dickens has been blamed for transferring so many actual incidents and sayings from his father's life into his sketch of Micawber ; but as the elder Dickens was just the man to laugh at his own troubles the moment they were past, and to enjoy a joke, even at his own expense, we may be sure that he would not consider the Micawber sketches as requiring either condemnation or excuse.

John Dickens was born in 1786, and in 1805 his name is found on the books of the pay-office of the Navy, in Somerset House, London, as seventh assistant clerk. Through Thomas Barrow, employed in the same establishment, he became acquainted with Elizabeth Barrow, whom he married on June 13th, 1809, in the church of St. Mary-in-the-Strand, only a few yards from Somerset House ; and soon after the marriage he was sent to Portsmouth. Here his first child, a daughter, was born in November 1810, and on November 23rd was christened Frances Elizabeth, a name which was afterwards contracted to Fanny.

On Friday, February 7th, 1812, a second child was born ; and on March 4th, at St. Mary's Church, was christened Charles John Huffham ; the last name being that of a maternal uncle, a " rigger to his

Majesty's Navy, Limehouse Hole." The house in which Fanny and Charles were born was No. 1, Mile End Terrace; also known as 387, Mile End Road, Landport; and here it may be well to state that Landport is one of the " four towns" which are generally known under the name of Portsmouth. The house still stands, unaltered, and in good repair; but the church of St. Mary was long since pulled down and re-built. The old font, slightly valued by St. Mary's, was re-placed by a new and more elaborate one, but fortunately for us it is preserved in the temporary church of

387, MILE END ROAD, LANDPORT.
Dickens's birthplace.

St. Stephen; and we hope that it will still be kept when the new St. Stephen's Church is built.

On the 24th of June, 1812, the Dickens family removed to Hawke Street, Portsea, so that it is a slight mistake to depict the youthful Charles as a little boy in petticoats in the front garden of the house in Mile End Terrace; although Forster, his biographer, states that he remembered the Hawke Street house. Even this is sufficient proof of precocity, since the family left Portsea in the winter of 1814, and lived for a few months in Norfolk Street, near the Middlesex Hospital, London.

Here occurs a short break in the history of the family; but we know certainly that in 1817 John Dickens occupied the house then

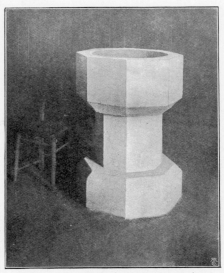

FONT FROM ST. MARY'S CHURCH, LANDPORT (NOW IN ST. STEPHEN'S CHURCH).
Dickens christened, March 4th, 1812.

known as No. 2 (now No. 11), Ordnance Terrace, Chatham. A brother of Charles, named Alfred, had been born at Hawke Street, and died in infancy; a sister, Letitia, was born in 1816; and a brother and a sister were born in the house in Ordnance Terrace, and christened at St. Mary's Church, Chatham. These were Harriet Ellen, christened September 3rd, 1819, who died in infancy, and Frederick William, christened August 4th, 1820.

Mr. Langton, in *The Childhood and Youth of Dickens*, has recorded very many interesting facts about this period; amongst them, that John Dickens's name frequently appeared on the lists of subscriptions raised for charitable and other purposes; and that his assistance on the relief committee formed after a great fire at Chatham earned the special and public thanks of the Treasurer of the fund. Mr. Langton also says that the account of this fire which appeared in *The Times* of March 4th, 1820, was written by John Dickens.

Although little Charles was but nine years old when he left Ordnance Terrace, he had already received a multitude of impressions which were afterwards to be worked into his writings. "The Old Lady" described in the second chapter of the *Sketches by Boz* was a Mrs. Newnham, who lived at No. 5 in the terrace, and the Half-pay Captain, described as living next door to her, was sketched from a retired officer who did live in Ordnance Terrace in Dickens's early days. George Stroughill, who lived at No. 1, and who was the greatest friend of little Charles, was unconsciously sitting for his portrait, as Steerforth, in *David Copperfield.* His name, distorted in boyish fun, is supposed to have suggested the name of Mr. Struggles, who, in Chapter VII. of *Pickwick*, is selected to bowl against "the hitherto unconquered Podder" in the cricket match at Muggleton.

Lucy Stroughill, the sister of George, was Dickens's childish sweetheart, a girl with blue eyes and golden hair, who gave her name to several characters in Dickens's works. In "Birthday Celebrations" (*Uncom. Trav.*, Chap. XIX.) we read: "I can very well remember being taken out to visit

HAWKE STREET, PORTSMOUTH (SECOND HOUSE). BY F. J. MORTIMER.
Dickens's home, 1812–1814.

some peach-faced creature in a blue sash and shoes to correspond, whose life I supposed to consist entirely of birthdays. . . At so early a stage of my travels did I assist at the anniversary of her nativity (and became enamoured of her), that I had not yet acquired the recondite knowledge that a birthday is the common property of all who are born, but supposed it to be a special gift bestowed by the favouring Heavens on that distinguished infant. There was no other company, and we sat in a shady bower —under a table, as my better (or worse) knowledge leads me to believe—and were regaled with saccharine substances and liquids, until it was time to depart."

In "Dullborough Town" (*Uncom. Trav*, Chap. XII.), we are told of a return to the scenes of boyhood: "Here, in the haymaking time, had I been delivered from the dungeons of Seringapatam, an immense pile (of haycocks), by my countrymen, the victorious British (boy next door and his two cousins), and had been recognised with ecstasy by my affianced one (Miss Green), who had come all the way from England (second house in the terrace) to ransom me, and

11, ORDNANCE TERRACE, CHATHAM (THE NEARER HOUSE).
Dickens's home, about 1817-1821.

marry me." This Miss Green of fiction was called Lucy ; and the uncommercial traveller tells that his old schoolfellow, Joe Specks, had married the same Lucy Green ; that when she appeared he was disappointed at the alteration in her face, but that when her youngest child came in, " I saw again the little face of the hay-field, unchanged, and it quite touched my foolish heart." That same " foolish heart " was to be charged with many such memories.

In " The Wreck of the Golden Mary " (*Christmas Stories*) Dickens speaks of another little Lucy, a child of three years old, of whom he says, " as the child had a quantity of shining fair hair, clustering in curls about her face, and as her name was Lucy, Steadiman gave her the name of 'the golden Lucy.'" And Lucie Manette (*Tale of Two Cities*) is described as " a young lady of short, slight, pretty figure, a quantity of golden hair, a pair of blue eyes." There are other Lucys, of less importance, on whom we need not dwell, and so much space has been given to this instance of childish memory only because it is a typical example of many early impressions kept through life.

Mary Weller was the servant of the Dickens family while they lived in Chatham, and from her Mr. Langton gleaned many facts about the novelist's boyhood. In particular, she said that he was carefully taught by his mother and his aunt ("Fanny") before he went to school, and was a great reader and reciter, even in those early days.

In 1821, John Dickens felt the need for financial retrenchment, and moved from Ordnance Terrace to a much smaller house, properly known as 18, St. Mary's Place, though St. Mary's Place is generally called "the Brook." This house still stands exactly as it did in those days, and from the window over the front door one can still look upon the burial-ground (now disused) which was in Dickens's mind when he wrote the very touching little sketch, "A Child's Dream of a Star" (*Reprinted Pieces*). "And so the time came all too soon when the child looked out alone;

ROCHESTER CASTLE.

"Ah! fine place—glorious pile—frowning walls—tottering arches—dark nooks—crumbling staircases."—*Pickwick*.

and when there was no face on the bed; and when there was a little grave among the graves not there before; and when the star made long rays down towards him, as he saw it through his tears."

Next door to the house on "the Brook" was, and still is, a chapel, in which officiated Mr. Giles, father of William Giles, who kept the first school to which Dickens was sent, and who was a good friend to the boy, even after his school-days. Only a few hundred yards away was the Church of St. Mary, where two children of John Dickens had already been christened, and where on April 3rd, 1822, another one was named Alfred Lamert, in honour of Matthew Lamert, Surgeon, who had on December 11th, 1821, in the same church married Dickens's aunt, Mary Allen (the aunt "Fanny" of the children). Dr. Lamert appeared in *Pickwick* as the irate Dr. Slammer. He already had a son, James, who took a great interest in little Charles, became his leader in walks and games, took him to the Theatre Royal at the foot of Star Hill, Rochester ; and even arranged private theatricals in which they both took some part. As will be seen in the next chapter, James Lamert became still more intimate with the Dickens family after their removal to London.

The Church of St. Mary, Chatham, still stands, at the time of writing, but its old and not very handsome pile is sandwiched between a new massive tower and an equally new, equally massive chancel, parts of a new church in which the old one will be entirely absorbed.

The Navy Yard, with the pay-office in which John Dickens worked, still remains, and still warrants the description given in *The Uncommercial Traveller*, Chapter XXIV. In his childish days Dickens knew it well, and with it he no doubt associated the "nurse's story" (*Uncom. Trav.*, XV.) which begins :—"There was once a shipwright, and he wrought in a Government Yard, and his name was Chips." Here also he may have seen the procession of blacksmiths and anchorsmiths on the day of their patron saint, Clement, and heard them lustily sing their processional song with the refrain which is given more than once in *Great Expectations* ; and of which Pip says, "the burden was Old Clem." This was not a very ceremonious way of rendering homage to a patron saint, but I believe Old Clem stood in that relation towards smiths. It was a

18, ST. MARY'S PLACE, CHATHAM (HOUSE NEXT TO CHAPEL).
Dickens's home, 1821-1823.

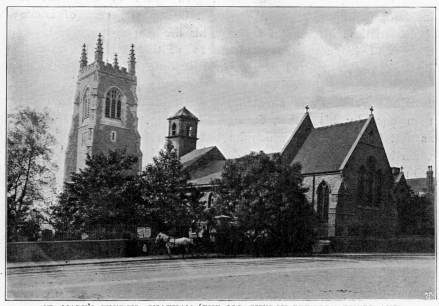

ST. MARY'S CHURCH, CHATHAM (THE OLD CHURCH BETWEEN TOWER AND
EAST END OF THE NEW).
Marriage and christenings in the Dickens family.

B

song that imitated the measure of beating upon iron, and was a mere lyrical excuse for the introduction of Old Clem's respected name. Thus, you were to "hammer boys round—Old Clem! With a thump and a sound—Old Clem! Beat it out, beat it out—Old Clem! With a clink for the stout—Old Clem!" and so forth. Just outside the Navy Yard lay one of the convict hulks which play their part in *Great Expectations.*

On the "Lines" at Chatham young Dickens must have often seen military manœuvres, just as Mr. Pickwick and his friends are said to have done : and he may have heard of duels in the field behind Fort Pitt, where Winkle went to meet Dr. Slammer. In the town was more than one old dealer in "marine stores" who might suggest the hideous old "Charley" to whom poor little David Copperfield sold his jacket for sixteen pence when he wearily tramped through Chatham on his way to Dover.

A host of recollections of Chatham are to be found in Dickens's various works, but here we must give space to only one more incident, an important one, because it illustrates several of Dickens's characteristics : his love of walking, his life-long memory of his early days, and his strong attachment to sentimental ideas. Chatham, Rochester, and Strood are practically one city, strung along a straggling street which forms a section of the great Dover Road from London. While quite a small boy he must have been taken more than once, by his father, through Rochester and Strood and as far as that Gadshill Place which he bought for his permanent residence when he had become a successful and wealthy man. In the chapter "On Travelling Abroad" an imaginary conversation with a "queer small boy" is reported :—

So smooth was the old high road, and so fresh were the horses, and so fast went I, that it was midway between Gravesend and Rochester, and the widening river was bearing the ships, white sailed or black-smoked, out to sea, when I noticed by the wayside a very queer small boy.

"Holloa," said I, to the very queer small boy, "where do you live ? "

"At Chatham," says he.

"What do you do there?" says I.

"I go to school," says he.

I took him up in a moment, and we went on. Presently the

KIT'S COTY HOUSE, NEAR MAIDSTONE.
Known to Dickens in his youth, and a favourite walk in later life.

very queer small boy says, "This is Gadshill we are coming to, where Falstaff went out to rob those travellers, and ran away."

"You know something about Falstaff, eh?" said I.

"All about him," said the very queer small boy. "I am old (I am nine), and I read all sorts of books. But do let us stop at the top of the hill, and look at the house there, if you please?"

"You admire that house?" said I.

"Bless you, sir," said the very queer small boy, "when I was not more than half as old as nine, it used to be a treat for me to be brought to look at it. And now I am nine, I come by myself to look at it. And ever since I can recollect, my father seeing me so fond of it, has often said to me, 'If you were to be very persevering and were to work hard, you might some day come to live in it.'

B 2

Though that's impossible!" said the very queer small boy, drawing a low breath, and now staring at the house out of the window with all his might.

Numerous as were the incidents and observations gathered during this childhood in Chatham and Rochester, the most valuable acquisition was the knowledge, and the taste for more knowledge, gained from the father's small library and from the stores of Mr. Giles. The very titles of his father's books show the almost morbid precocity in the young child who read them over and over again, for they included, *Roderick Random*, *Peregrine Pickle*, *Humphrey Clinker*, *Tom Jones*, *The Vicar of Wakefield*, *Don Quixote*, *Gil Blas*, *Robinson Crusoe*, *The Arabian Nights*, *The Spectator*, *The Idler*, *The Humourist's Miscellany*, *The Tatler*, *Tales of the Genii*, *The Citizen of the World*, and a collection of Farces. These works stimulated his imagination, and laid the foundation of his style. Even before leaving Chatham, he wrote a tragedy, *Misnar, the Sultan of India*: founded on one of the *Tales of the Genii*.

ROAD THROUGH COBHAM PARK.

" Through a deep and shady wood, cooled by the light wind which gently rustled the thick foliage."—*Pickwick*.

CHAPTER II

Boyhood and Youth in London. 1823—1831

"Heart of London, there is a moral in thy every stroke! as I look on at thy indomitable working, which neither death, nor press of life, not grief, not gladness out of doors will influence one jot, I seem to hear a voice within thee which sinks into my heart, bidding me, as I elbow my way among the crowd, have some thought for the meanest wretch that passes, and, being a man, to turn away with scorn and pride from none that bear the human shape."

A FRAGILE child, with an ever-busy brain poorly sustained by a delicate, high-strung physical frame, was little Charles Dickens, and it may have been some temporary illness which caused him to be left, for a time, in the care of Mr. Giles when his father and the rest of the family left Chatham for London. This removal was probably, if not quite certainly, in the winter of 1822–23, and the family travelled to London by coach, sending their furniture by water. This would mean a delay of at least a few days before the furniture could be placed in the new home, and would probably involve some days of discomfort in cheap lodgings or

TIMPSON'S
"BLUE-EYED
MAID."

in an almost unfurnished house, for John Dickens was oppressed with debt, so that he could not think of staying in an expensive and comfortable hotel. The family settled in No. 141, Bayham Street, Camden Town; a small house in a cheap neighbourhood. The locality was not quite so poor as it is now, but even then it was chosen for economy rather than for comfort. From Forster we gather that Charles did not associate with the boys of the neighbourhood any more than did his parents with the washerwoman who lived next door or the Bow-Street officer over the way.

Of Dickens's journey down from Chatham to London we are told in "Dullborough Town" (*Uncom. Trav.*, XII.):—"As I left Dullborough in the days when there were no railroads in the land, I left it in a coach. Through all the years that have since passed, have I ever lost the smell of the damp straw in which I was packed—like game—and forwarded, carriage paid, to the 'Cross Keys,' Wood Street, Cheapside, London? There was no other inside passenger, and I consumed my sandwiches in solitude and dreariness, and it rained hard all the way, and I thought life sloppier than I had expected to find it." He says that the coach was Timpson's Blue-Eyed Maid, which may have been an actual fact, since a Blue-Eyed Maid did run from Chatham, and was owned by a livery-man called Simpson.

The depressing stage-coach journey was the beginning of an experience of discomfort and neglect, such as might have broken the spirit of a boy with Dickens's sensitiveness if it had not been for his strong natural optimism and his sense of humour. The family pride which prevented his mixing in the sports of such boys of his own age as lived near his new home, combined with a poverty which kept his parents busy and anxious, forced him upon his own resources; and these, in a comfortless home in a poor district, without a single friendly neighbour, were very slight. From sheer preoccupation, as it seems, John Dickens neglected to send his son to any school, and the poor boy's feelings have been described in his own words, preserved to us by Forster. He prefaces them by an eloquent testimony to his father's kindness, and adds: "But, in

the ease of his temper and the straightness of his means, he appeared
to have utterly lost at this time the idea of educating me at all,

NO. 141 (FORMERLY 16), BAYHAM STREET, CAMDEN TOWN.
"A mean, small tenement with a wretched little back garden."—Forster's *Life*.

and to have utterly put from him the notion that I had any claim
upon him, in that regard, whatever. So I degenerated into cleaning
his boots of a morning, and my own ; and making myself useful in
the work of the little house, and looking after my younger brothers
and sisters (we were now six in all), and going on such poor errands as
arose out of our poor way of living. . . . As I thought, in the little
back attic of Bayham Street, of all I had lost in losing Chatham,
what would I have given, if I had had anything to give, to have
been sent back to any other school, to have been taught something
anywhere."

A picture of the district, when it was in a state of convulsion
owing to the building of the North Western Railway close to it, is

given in Chapter IV. of *Dombey and Son*, in the description of Staggs's Gardens. Near here Dickens located Boffin's Bower, the home of the Golden Dustman (*Mutual Friend*, Chapter V.). Its site has been covered by the great network of steel over which the traffic of the Midland and the Great Northern railways enters London, and nothing remains of those "dust heaps and dock leaves and fields" over which the boy Dickens used to look "at the cupola of St. Paul's looming through the smoke, a treat that served him for hours of vague reflection afterwards."

The house occupied by the Dickens family was No. 16 (now re-numbered 141) and was only a cottage, recently built, and with much open space and fields around it. It was one of a row of a dozen or so, each of them having a little back garden or yard with enclos-ing wall, as may still be seen. At the top of Bayham Street, says Forster, were some almshouses. Perhaps this is a slip of memory, but at any rate there is still on the east side of Bayham Street, a little lower down than No. 141, a row of almshouses which may have suggested the chapter on Titbull's Almshouses (*Uncom. Trav.*, XXVII.), though Dickens describes Titbull's as being in the east of London ; and which very probably were in his mind when he wrote (in *Dombey*) of the Charitable Grinders.

In *David Copperfield*, which is very largely a history of Dickens's own experiences, many of the incidents of this miserable period are given. The description of the house in which Mr. Micawber lived with Traddles as a lodger, exactly fits the house in Bayham Street, and possibly even such details as the angry behaviour of the milkman with the unpaid bill were founded upon fact. The "very youthful servant girl" was, at any rate, no creature of the imagination, for on leaving Chatham the Dickens family had brought with them an orphan (or as she had it, an "orfling") girl from the workhouse there,—whose portrait was given as "the Marchioness" in *The Old Curiosity Shop*. She served the family very faithfully, and remained with them through their worst misfortunes.

To add to his other miseries, little Charles was still far from robust; he was small for his age, pinched in appearance, and subject to frequent illnesses. The final blow seemed to fall when, although he was not allowed to go to school, his sister Fanny was sent to an expensive Academy of Music. But there were some bright spots in the dark picture, and most of these were supplied through the kindness and sympathy of James Lamert, who became a member of the family soon after their settlement in Bayham Street. He had been studying at the military college of Sandhurst, and while waiting for the commission he hoped to receive, had little or nothing to do. To while away the hours indoors he made a toy theatre, with painted scenes and miniature actors, which gave much pleasure to his young friend. More than this, he took the little lad to walk in those wonderful mazes of streets around Seven Dials, Covent Garden, Drury Lane, and the Adelphi; places made the more fascinating by their reputation for vice and absolute lawlessness.

During this period Charles visited his godfather, Mr. Huffam, the rigger in Limehouse, probably now making his first acquaintance with the Wooden Midshipman (*Dombey*), and certainly with many of the waterside surroundings of Captain Cuttle, of Rogue Riderhood, and of the convict, Magwitch. He also visited his mother's brother, Thomas Barrow, then living in Gerrard Street, Soho, who lent him a number of books.

The financial troubles of the father were steadily increasing; and a certain "deed" in connection with an attempted composition with the creditors became prominent in the family councils, and assumed, to the boy who only partly understood its meaning, a very terrific shape. The creditors did not accept the composition, and it was felt that some great effort must be made. It was suggested that Mrs. Dickens should open a school for young ladies, for which purpose the family removed to No. 4, Gower Street North (since destroyed to make room for a furniture warehouse), where a large brass plate was fixed on the door to announce Mrs. Dickens's Establishment. It was expected that Mr. Huffam, who was supposed to have great connections in the merchant-trade to the East, could introduce a number of children sent from India to be educated. Charles was sent out to deliver circulars to many houses in the neighbourhood, but beyond this no effort was made, and the words used in reference to Mrs. Micawber's "establishment" (*Copperfield*,

A RIGGER'S SHOP, "DOWN LIMEHOUSE WAY."

Chap. XI.) were literally from sad experience :—" I never found that any young lady had ever been to school there ; or that any young lady ever came, or proposed to come ; or that the least preparation was ever made to receive any young lady. The only visitors I saw or heard of were creditors. *They* used to come at all hours, and some of them were quite ferocious." The story of this unfortunate attempt is completed by a few words recorded in *Our Mutual Friend* (Chap. IV.) as having been uttered by Mrs. Wilfer :—" Yes, the man came himself with a pair of pincers, and took it off, and took it away. He said that as he had no expectation of ever being paid for it, and as he had another order for a *Ladies' School* door-plate, it was better (burnished up) for the interests of all parties."

Almost the whole of the incidents related in Chapters XI. and XII. of *David Copperfield* are given exactly as they occurred to the real Charles Dickens, and are a compound of the life in Bayham Street and in Gower Street. James Lamert who had lodged with the Dickens family, had joined a cousin, George Lamert, whose business was the making of a Warren's Blacking to rival the older-established Warren in the same trade. Jonathan Warren, who started the Lamerts in the business, said that he was the rightful owner of

GRAY'S INN GARDENS.

Well known to Dickens when employed in Gray's Inn, and when living in Furnival's Inn and Doughty Street.

the recipe for the blacking, and that he had been in some way defrauded of his rights; wherefore, as the successful (Robert) Warren traded from 30, Strand, the opposition took premises at 30, Hungerford Stairs, Strand, and printed their bottle-labels with 30, Strand, very large and "Hungerford Stairs" very small. The competition was keen and unscrupulous, and as there was no copyright law to protect advertisements, one firm exactly copied the pictorial announcements of the other. Here Charles began work, at six or seven shillings a week, and suffered those humiliations and mortifications which he connects with the Murdstone and Grinby business in *Copperfield*.

Filling and labelling pots of blacking is not a very refined occupation, but Dickens, like Copperfield, was acknowledged by the other boys as their social superior except on one occasion, when "Mealy Potatoes uprose once, and rebelled against my being so distinguished, but Mick Walker settled him in no time." The corresponding passage from real life reads:—"Poll Green uprose once, and rebelled against the 'young gentleman' usage, but Bob Fagin settled him speedily;" and it is interesting to notice that the real names of his boyish companions were used later, Fagin in *Oliver Twist*, and Poll (with the invented surname Sweedlepipe) in *Martin Chuzzlewit*.

So sensitive was Charles to the indignity of his position that in writing to Forster, years afterwards, he says that that phase of his life had never been alluded to, even with his father or mother or his wife, and he adds,—"until old Hungerford Stairs were destroyed and the very nature of the ground changed, I never had the courage to go back to the place where my servitude began. I never saw it. I could not endure to go near it. For many years, when I came near to Robert Warren's in the Strand, I crossed over to the opposite side of the way to avoid a certain smell of the cement they put upon the blacking corks, which reminded me of what I once was. It was a very long time before I liked to go up Chandos Street. My old way home by the Borough made me cry, after my eldest child could speak." No wonder that trials felt so keenly should be touchingly recorded in *David Copper-field*. No wonder that the boy who suffered poverty and degrada-tion should make a man sympathetic to every phase of human wretchedness.

Before very long, the creditors became so pressing that Mr. Dickens was arrested for debt, and taken away to one of those sponging houses of which his son has given us so many pictures, and which his writings did so much to improve off the face of the earth. Charles was employed by his father to run errands to persons who might be expected to render some aid ; and by his mother to pawn or sell all the portable belongings. He was sent many times to a second-hand bookseller in Hampstead Road, just as Copperfield is said to have been sent to one in City Road ; as well as to a pawnbroker's in the same locality. Such furniture as was too heavy to be dealt with in this way was taken away in a van, with the exception of "a few chairs, a kitchen table, and some beds," and, to quote from *Copperfield*, "we encamped, as it were, in the two parlours of the emptied house, . . . Mrs. Micawber, the children, the orfling, and myself; and lived in these rooms night and day."

Mr. Dickens, unable to raise the necessary money for his release, was removed to one of the debtors' prisons, and here comes a little conflict of evidence. Forster says that this prison was the Marshalsea ; but he makes the slip of saying, "The readers of Mr. Micawber's history who remember David's first visit to the Marshalsea," etc. Mr. Micawber's prison is said to have been the King's Bench ; and Mr. Robert Langton has unearthed the fact, which he records in his *Childhood and Youth of Dickens*, that during the time when John Dickens was in *one* of the debtors' prisons, a Mr. Dorrett (of Rochester) was confined in the King's Bench. This may have been the source of the name used in *Little Dorrit* for the prisoner of the Marshalsea. On the other hand, Forster quotes from a personal statement of Dickens, "written two or three years before the fiction (*David Copperfield*) had even entered into his thoughts," the following details : "My father was waiting for me in the lodge, and we went up to his room (on the top story but one) and cried very much. And he told me, I remember, to take warning by the Marshalsea, and to observe that if a man had twenty pounds a year, and spent nineteen pounds, nineteen shillings, and sixpence, he would be happy; but that a shilling spent the other way would make him wretched." An almost exact replica of this little financial sermon is placed in the mouth of Micawber. Meanwhile there is another piece of evidence as to the debtors' prison in which John Dickens was confined; and like the last mentioned, it is quoted by Forster as if from

LANT STREET, BOROUGH.
"A repose about Lant Street that sheds a gentle melancholy upon the soul."—*Pickwick.*

Dickens's definite statement. It relates how the boy, who was then lodging in North London, complained to his father of his isolation from the rest of the family, and how, in order that he might be near the prison, "a back attic was found for me at the house of an insolvent-court agent, who lived in Lant Street, in the Borough, where Bob Sawyer lodged many years afterwards." As the end of Lant Street is within a few yards of the Marshalsea prison, this statement seems to fully support Forster.

Before moving into Lant Street lodgings Dickens had been sent, when his mother and the rest of the family joined his father in the prison, to live with a Mrs. Roylance in Little College Street, Camden Town, very near the Bayham Street house. He writes of this lady as one "who took children in to board, and had once done so at Brighton; and who, with a few alterations and embellishments, unconsciously began to sit for Mrs. Pipchin in *Dombey*."

All this time, Fanny Dickens was a boarder at the Academy of Music, whence she was fetched every Sunday by her brother Charles that they might walk to the prison, and spend the day there. While living in Lant Street, Charles went every morning to the prison to breakfast with the family, and as he was often astir long before the gates were open, he sometimes met and walked with the little servant who was to become "The Orfling" and "the Marchioness," and who, like himself, had a lodging near the prison. Forster says, "when Charles met her, as he would do occasionally, in his lounging-place by London Bridge, he would occupy the time before the gates opened by telling her quite astonishing fictions about

NO. 13 (FORMERLY 29), JOHNSON STREET.
Identified in Kitton's *Life* as Dickens's home about 1824.

the wharves and the Tower." We think it probable that "the Iron Bridge" (Southwark Bridge) was the Dickens lounging-place. In *Little Dorrit* (Chap. IX.) he represents Clennam as saying to Little Dorrit, "Will you go by the Iron Bridge, where there is an escape from the noise of the street?" and in Chap. XVIII. he further says to Young John, "Amy has gone for an airing on the Iron Bridge. She has become quite partial to the Iron Bridge of late, and seems to like to walk there better than anywhere."

The insolvent-court agent, with whom Dickens lodged, was very kind to the boy, as were his wife and son, and in *The Old Curiosity*

Shop they appear as the Garland family. For all that, Dickens keenly felt the disgrace of his position, and on one occasion when he had been seriously ill during the afternoon and the kindly Bob

NO. 18, BENTINCK STREET (DARK HOUSE NEAR RIGHT).
Dickens's home, 1828–1834.

Fagin insisted on accompanying him home he resorted to subterfuge to hide the truth. After trying by various means to get rid of Fagin, Dickens shook hands with him on the steps of a good house, and knocked at the door. When it was opened he inquired if Mr. Robert Fagin lived there, and by this means gained time for his companion to get out of sight.

During this period one of the chief pleasures of Dickens's life was the walk to his lodgings on Saturday night when he had a few pence, and when the market streets were at their brightest and busiest. At such times he went over Blackfriars Bridge, along a road which abounded in busy cheap shops, with occasional showrooms in which the public were invited to examine the fat pig, the wild Indian, or the dwarf lady. In the dinner-hour he used to wander through the mysterious labyrinths of the Durham Arches, under the Adelphi Terrace and neighbouring streets, coming out upon the low water-side quarters which have

been swept away by the building of the Thames Embankment, but
which were then the resorts of bargemen and coal-heavers engaged
in the river-side traffic.   Another district that never lost its charm
of mingled attraction and re-
pulsion was Covent Garden, of
which Dickens says in Forster,
" when I had no money [for a
meal] I took a turn in Covent
Garden Market, and stared at
the pine-apples."   In *Little
Dorrit* (Chapter XIV.) the childish vision of Covent Garden is
given in these words : " Courtly
ideas of Covent Garden, as a
place with famous coffee-houses,
where gentlemen wearing gold-
laced coats and swords had
quarrelled and fought duels ;
costly ideas of Covent Garden
as a place where there were
flowers in winter at guineas
a-piece, pine-apples at guineas
a pound, and peas at guineas
a pint ; picturesque ideas of

SEYMOUR STREET CHAPEL.
" We very piously attended the morning service."—
Dr. Danson in Forster's *Life*.

Covent Garden, as a place where there was a mighty theatre,
showing wonderful and beautiful sights to richly-dressed ladies and
gentlemen, and which was for ever far beyond the reach of poor
Fanny or poor uncle ; desolate ideas of Covent Garden, as having
all those arches in it, where the miserable children in rags among
whom she had just now passed, like young rats, slunk and hid, fed
on offal, huddled together for warmth, and were hunted about ;
teeming ideas of Covent Garden, as a place of past and present
mystery, romance, abundance, want, beauty, ugliness, fair country
gardens, and foul street gutters, all confused together."

How John Dickens satisfied his superiors in the Navy Office, or

C

how his work was done during his imprisonment, we do not know, but his salary continued to be paid, so that the family was in better circumstances for the forced cessation of the attempt to satisfy

WELLINGTON HOUSE ACADEMY.
"A school of some celebrity in its neighbourhood,—nobody could have said why."—*Our School*.

creditors. A new deed of arrangement was offered, but after much negotiation the creditors refused to accept it, and the only alternative was to file a petition under the Insolvent Debtors Act. This secured the release of the prisoner, free from his burdens, and in a happier state of mind than had been possible for some years. They first went to lodge for a time with Mrs. Roylance (Mrs. Pipchin) in Little College Street, and afterwards settled in Johnson Street, Somers Town, at No. 29 (now No. 13). This was but a short distance from Mrs. Roylance's and from Bayham Street.

The worst troubles were over. Dickens says,—"Now, I generally had my dinner at the warehouse. Sometimes I brought it from home, so I was better off. I see myself coming across Russell Square from Somers Town, one morning, with some cold hotch-potch in a basin tied up in a handkerchief. I had the same wanderings

about the streets as I used to have, and was just as solitary and
self-dependent as before; but I had not the same difficulty in merely
living." The feeling of humiliation remained, however, with the long-
ing for more learning, and for the society of some one more refined
than Bob Fagin and Poll Green.
Of an occasion when he attended a prize-giving at the
Academy of Music to see his
sister Fanny receive an award
he says,—" I could not bear to
think of myself beyond the
reach of all such honourable
emulation and success. The
tears ran down my face. I felt
as if my heart were rent. I
prayed, when I went to bed
that night, to be lifted out of
the humiliation and neglect in
which I was. I never had
suffered so much before. There
was no envy in this."

GATEWAY OF LINCOLN'S INN.
" We passed into sudden quietude under an old gateway."
—*Bleak House.*

The old blacking-warehouse
in Hungerford Stairs has gone: and the place to which the business
was removed and where Charles spent the latter part of his servitude
(at the corner of Bedford and Chandos Streets) has also disappeared;
—it is perhaps well that the principal remaining relic of this dark
period should be the Marshalsea prison, around which Dickens was
able to weave so many humorous and tender memories.

The bankruptcy petition was filed on May 4th, 1824, and the
first hearing was on May 27th. Most likely the discharge from the
prison came soon after, and probably it was during the summer of
this year that Charles, after a quarrel between his father and James
Lamert, about the menial nature of his work, was removed from
the blacking factory. He was sent to the Wellington House
Academy, in a building which still stands at the corner of

C 2

Hampstead Road and Granby Street.   The school-room, a one-story continuation, has been removed in the construction of the London and North-Western Railway, but it formerly ran along the side of Granby Street, and was surrounded by a large yard.   Here Dickens stayed until Christmas of 1825, gathering experiences which he seems to have blended with those of Mr. Giles's school at Chatham.   Both Forster and Langton have preserved reminiscences by his school-fellows, one of whom says that " He usually held his head more erect than lads ordinarily do, and there was a general smart-ness about him."   Another says :—" He was a hand-some, curly-headed lad, full of animation and animal spirits, and probably was connected with every mis-chievous prank in the school."

GRAY'S INN GATEWAY : HOLBORN.
" Job Trotter ran up Holborn regardless of obstacles, until he
reached the gate of Gray's Inn."—*Pickwick*.

The establishment seems to have been fairly well officered, for, in addition to the principal, there were Latin, English, Junior, and French masters.   In *Our School* (Re-printed Pieces), Dickens says :—" It was a school of some celebrity in its neighbourhood—nobody could have said why—and we had the honour to attain and hold the eminent position of first boy. The master was supposed among us to know nothing, and one of the ushers was supposed to know everything. We are still inclined to think the first-named supposition perfectly correct." This ignorant head master was one Mr. Jones, a Welshman, who is supposed to be the original of Mr. Creakle, in *David Copperfield*. Mr. Taylor, the English master, played the flute, and was doubtless the original of Copperfield's Mr. Mell. The "serving-man, whose name was Phil," and who, "when we had the scarlet fever in the school, nursed all the sick boys of his own accord, and was like a mother to them" (*Our School*), was an actual attendant at Wellington House, and he seems to have favourably impressed Dickens with his kindness during the boys' illness, for he again appears in *Bleak House* as that Phil Squod, who, "with his smoky gunpowder visage, at once acts as nurse and works as armourer" when poor Jo is dying in Mr. George's shooting-gallery.

SOUTH SQUARE (FORMERLY HOLBORN COURT) GRAY'S INN.
"Mr. Traddles lives in . . . . Holborn Court, Number Two."
—*Copperfield.*

Amongst the pupils at Wellington House was Beverley, afterwards a noted scene painter, with whom Dickens entered into a partnership for the construction of a miniature theatre and the production of plays. Amongst the boarders were three of the name of Key. Their sisters also lived in the house, and as they were mulattoes sent from the East Indies, it is probable they suggested the characters of Neville and Helena Landless in *Edwin Drood*. The *Schoolboy's*

Story (Reprinted Pieces) describes the incidents at this school, though the name of its hero, "Old Cheeseman," is taken from a schoolfellow at Chatham.

After leaving school (the exact date is not certain) Dickens obtained employment with Mr. Molloy, a solicitor in New Square,

FIELD COURT, GRAY'S INN.

"I was surprised by meeting a lively leech ; seemingly on his way to the West End."—*Chambers* (*Uncom. Trav.*).

Lincoln's Inn. The hall of Lincoln's Inn became the scene of the great Jarndyce trial (*Bleak House*). Old Square, Lincoln's Inn, held the offices of Sergeant Snubbin (*Pickwick*), as also of Kenge and Carboy, solicitors to Mr. Jarndyce (*Bleak House*). Of Dickens's service here very little is known. It was not long, however, before he left Lincoln's Inn for Gray's Inn, to enter the office of Ellis and Blackmore, where he worked from May, 1827, to November, 1828. A curious relic of this connection is the firm's petty cash book, kept by Dickens himself while in their employ, and containing many names which afterwards did duty in his works, in but slightly altered form. Mr. Blackmore has stated that some of the incidents mentioned in *Pickwick* and in *Nickleby* actually took place while Dickens was with him ; and that some of the characters were evidently based on persons he knew there.

The old chambers in Gray's Inn remain much as they were in Dickens's time, and still stumbling up a dark stairway we may recall Mr. Pickwick's visit to Mr. Perker's chambers. "After climbing two pairs of steep and dirty stairs," and vainly kicking Mr. Perker's door, Sam Weller said :

"Here's an old 'ooman comin' up-stairs, sir, p'raps she knows where we can find somebody. Hallo, old lady, vere's Mr. Perker's people ? "

"Mr. Perker's people ; . . . Mr. Perker's people's gone, and I'm a-goin' to do the office out."

"Are you Mr. Perker's servant ? " inquired Mr. Pickwick.

"I am Mr. Perker's laundress."

And still on the old stairs of these and other chambers we may meet the "old 'ooman goin' to do the office out," and may find that she prefers to be called a laundress rather than a servant.

While in Ellis and Blackmore's office, Dickens and a fellow-clerk, named Potter, spent much of their spare time (and cash) in patronising those "Private Theatres," which he describes with such humour and such intimate knowledge in Chapter XIII. of *Boz*. Though the particular "gaff," affected by Charles and his companion, has doubtless long since disappeared, there are still such places to be found by those who know their London well, where ladies of the millinery profession, junior clerks, and young tradesmen (for lawyer's clerks are now *much* above such things) pay for the privilege of taking leading parts, and where the placard may still be seen in the gentlemen's dressing-room :—"Richard the Third, Duke of Glo'ster, £2 ; Earl of Richmond, £1 ; Duke of Buckingham, 15s. ; Catesby, 12s. ; Tressel, 10s. 6d. ; Lord Stanley, 5s. ; Lord Mayor of London, 2s. 6d."

It is uncertain when Dickens's thoughts first turned to newspaper reporting as a possible means of better livelihood than he could gain as a clerk. The suggestion came from his father's success in mastering shorthand, and securing a position as reporter for *The Morning Herald* in the gallery of the House of Commons, and it was while clerk with Ellis and Blackmore that he studied *Gurney's Brachygraphy*, "an Easy and Compendious System of Shorthand," which plunged him into "a sea of perplexity that brought me in a few weeks to the confines of distraction." Although David Copperfield, who is so largely a portrait of Dickens's self at this time, speaks of learning shorthand as an occupation taken up while engaged at Doctors' Commons, it was Dickens's knowledge of the art which led to his employment at Doctors' Commons as a writer to the Proctors at the end of 1828. Forster hints that (as in the case of Copperfield) there was a love affair to spur on the young wrestler with the difficulties of shorthand.

GRAY'S INN ROAD ENTRANCE TO GRAY'S INN.
" Mrs. Perker's laundress lived . . . somewhere behind
Gray's Inn Lane."—*Pickwick*.

Certain it is that Dickens thoroughly "tamed that savage stenographic mystery," for a master of the craft has said of him, "there never *was* such a shorthand writer;" and equally certain it is that the engagement in Doctors' Commons was only accepted as temporary work until a better opening should appear. Of the attachment to "Dora" which was the incentive to this work we may quote what Dickens wrote to Forster in 1855, about his youthful passion: "that it excluded every other idea from my mind for four years, . . and that I went at it with a determination to overcome all the difficulties, which fairly lifted me up into that newspaper life, and floated me away over a hundred men's heads."

Although studying shorthand, Dickens was not neglecting any of the other opportunities for self-improvement that chance threw in his way; and the very day after attaining the necessary age of eighteen he made his first attendance as a reader at the British Museum, a library which he afterwards used very frequently.

DEAN'S COURT, DOCTORS' COMMONS.
"When I was a shorthand writer to the Proctors."—Forster's *Life*.

Restless in the Doctors' Commons, uncertain of ever securing a good newspaper post, Dickens, in his nineteenth year, seriously turned his thoughts to the stage as an avenue to position and competence, and took all possible steps, by attending performances, and by studying and rehearsing parts, to fit himself for a theatrical life. His sister Fanny helped him in the matter, and accompanied his singing parts; and at one time he went so far as to approach the management of Covent Garden Theatre, in a letter which secured an appointment for him to show his ability. Illness prevented his keeping the appointment, which was postponed to the next season; and meanwhile, the longed-for newspaper opening appeared, so that ideas of the stage were abandoned.

During this part of his life Dickens lived with his father, first in Johnson Street, then at Bentinck Street, Manchester Square (a house which was pulled down in 1902), and later, at No. 10, Norfolk Street, Fitzroy Square, which is the address entered on his reader's ticket at the British Museum.

THE COLLEGE, COBHAM (NOW USED AS ALMS-HOUSES).

"This is some very old inscription, existing perhaps long before the ancient alms-houses in this place."—*Pickwick*.

CHAPTER III

Newspaper Work, and "Sketches by Boz"

LONDON, IPSWICH, BATH, BRISTOL,
ETC., 1831—1836

YOUNG DICKENS as he was soon to be familiarly called by London press-men, secured in 1831 a post as Parliamentary reporter for *The True Sun*, through which he first became acquainted with John Forster, who was afterwards to become his closest friend and his biographer. The meeting was peculiar. Forster was friendly with certain members of the editorial staff, and helped them through some of their difficulties, which included a general strike of the reporters. At this time, Forster met on the stairs of the office, "a young man of my own age, whose keen animation of look would have arrested attention anywhere." This proved to be "young Dickens," who "had been spokesman for the recalcitrant reporters and conducted their case triumphantly."

SARACEN'S HEAD, BATH.

Small as the incident is, it shows that even the "blacking-bottle period" had not crushed Dickens's spirit. He was keenly sensitive to anything he deemed unjust, quite ready to lead in attacking the abuse, and his comrades, to whom he cannot have been very well known, recognised him as a suitable champion. This same early recognition of his merits is shown by a fact related to us only a few years ago by the veteran composer, the late Henry Russell. When he was a young ambitious musician, Russell was friendly with Mr. George Hogarth, who one day brought him the words of a

PART OF MS. OF "THE IVY GREEN," COPIED FOR MRS. WARD BY THE COMPOSER.

song, saying that it was the work of a very promising young writer, and suggesting that he should set it to music. The song was *The Ivy Green*, which was not published in *Pickwick* until some time later, after Mr. Russell had set it to the beautiful melody which is still its best accompaniment.

Through the Parliamentary session of 1831 Dickens reported for *The True Sun*; during 1832 and 1833 he similarly represented *The Mirror of Parliament*, which was established by his uncle, Thomas Barrow, and claimed to surpass "Hansard" as a report of the doings of the "House"; and later, in 1833, he joined the staff of *The Morning Chronicle*, then being published at No. 332, Strand, in a substantial building which remained intact until it was swept away by the Holborn-Strand improvements in 1902. Of this period, and in reference to his stage aspirations, Dickens afterwards wrote: "I made a great splash in the gallery, . . the *Chronicle* opened to me; I had a distinction in the little world of newspaper, which

OFFICE OF "THE MORNING CHRONICLE": 332, STRAND, LONDON.

Dickens joined the staff in 1833.

made one like it; began to write; didn't want money; had never thought of the stage but as a means of getting it; gradually left off turning my thoughts that way, and never resumed the idea."

FURNIVAL'S INN, HOLBORN.
The gateway and the houses on to which Dickens's windows looked.

The reporting in Parliament gave good training, and established habits of neatness, quickness, accuracy, and self-reliance, attributes often wanting in people of Dickens's spontaneous genius, and which contributed much to his success. The work of *The Morning Chronicle*, which took him far away from London, on flying excursions to report great political speeches, gave a vent to his unbounded energy and brought him into touch with many a scene which was to live in his works. It is worthy of note that the earliest letter now remaining from his hand refers to a reporting drive into Essex and Suffolk; and that another of these very early excursions was to Bath and Bristol, all of which figure so largely in *Pickwick*. The letter in which he mentions his journey into Essex was written to Mr. Henry Austin, who afterwards married his sister Letitia, and is so characteristic that it may well be quoted in full (from *The Letters of Charles Dickens*).

Furnival's Inn, Wednesday night, past 12.

DEAR HENRY,

I have just been ordered on a journey, the length of which is at present uncertain. I may be back on Sunday very probably,

FURNIVAL'S INN, LOOKING TOWARD HOLBORN.

" Your rest must be provided for, and you shall have the prettiest chamber in Furnival's."—*Ed. Drooa.*

and start again on the following day. Should this be the case, you shall hear from me before.

Don't laugh. I am going (alone) in a gig ; and, to quote the eloquent inducement which the proprietors of Hampstead *chays* hold out to Sunday riders, "the gen't'm'n drives himself." I am going into Essex and Suffolk. It strikes me I shall be spilt before I pay a turnpike. I have a presentiment I shall run over an only child before I reach Chelmsford, my first stage.

Let the evident haste of this specimen of "The Polite Letter Writer" be its excuse, and

Believe me, dear Henry, most sincerely yours,

CHARLES DICKENS.

In this journey Dickens probably drove along Aldgate past the famous pump, past the Bull Inn, Whitechapel (long since pulled

WHITECHAPEL HIGH STREET ("BUTCHERS' ROW").
" I shall work down to Ipswich the day arter to-morrow, from the Bull in Whitechapel."—*Pickwick*.

down), whence Mr. Pickwick started for Ipswich (Chap. XXII.); up the Whitechapel High Street, which still has its long range of quaint old shops known as "Butchers' Row," and its hay and straw market held in the open street three days a week; through the turnpike at the Mile End, which began the Mile End Road, and past the quaint old Vines public-house, which still stands at the time of writing, but which is very shortly to be pulled down for rebuilding. Even to this day the wide open space beside the roadway, paved to

Mile End, and gravelled beyond, is a great market for oysters, whelks, and winkles, which are vended from stalls, much as they were when Sam Weller said, "It's a wery remarkable circumstance, sir, that poverty and oysters always seems to go together," and

CORNER OF COMMERCIAL STREET AND FLOWER STREET, WHITECHAPEL.

"The Self-supporting Cooking Depot had hired a newly-built warehouse."—"*Boiled Beef of New England*," *Uncom. Trav.*

further, "What I mean, sir, is, that the poorer a place is, the greater call there seems to be for oysters. Look here, sir, here's a oyster stall to every half-dozen houses—the street's lined vith 'em. Blessed if I don't think that ven a man's wery poor, he rushes out of his lodgings, and eats oysters in reg'lar desperation." "To be sure he does," said Mr. Weller, senior, "and it's just the same vith pickled salmon."

In connection with these journeys by post-chaise, coach, and gig, Dickens's thoroughness, resourcefulness, and energy came well to the front, and he told Forster (in speaking of the splendid way in which

D

the proprietors of the *Chronicle* supported him) how he had had to charge them for "half-a-dozen break-downs in half-a-dozen times as many miles; for damage to a great-coat from drippings of wax candles; for all sorts of breakages, such being the ordinary result of

GREAT CORAM STREET.

"Mrs. Tibbs was the most tidy, fidgety, thrifty little personage, and the house was the neatest in Great Coram Street."—*Sketches*.

the pace which we went at. I have charged for broken hats, broken luggage, broken chaises, broken harness, everything but a broken head, which is the only thing they would have grumbled to pay for." Speaking as Chairman at a Dinner of the Newspaper Press Fund, held at the Freemason's Tavern, May 20, 1865, he said:—"I have often transcribed for the printer, from my shorthand notes, important public speeches in which the strictest accuracy was required, and a mistake in which would have been to a young man severely compromising, writing on the palm of my hand, by the light of a dark lantern, in a post-chaise and four, galloping through a wild country, and through the dead of the night, at the then

(NEW) ST. PANCRAS CHURCH.

"The clock of St. Pancras Church struck twelve, and the Foundling, with laudable politeness, did the same ten minutes afterwards."—"*Our Boarding House*," *Sketches*.

D 2

surprising rate of fifteen miles an hour. . . Returning home from excited political meetings in the country to the waiting press in London, I do verily believe I have been upset in almost every description of vehicle known in this country. I have been belated on miry by-roads, towards the small hours, forty or fifty miles from London, in a wheelless carriage, with exhausted horses and drunken post-boys, and have got back in time for publication, to be received with never-forgotten compliments by the late Mr. Black, coming in the broadest of Scotch from the broadest of hearts I ever knew."

WHITECHAPEL WORKHOUSE.

"Against the house were leaning what seemed to be seven heaps of rags,
'dumb, wet, silent horrors' he described them."—Forster's *Life*.

Dickens's reporting trip to Bath and Bristol was undertaken in May, 1835, for the reporting of Lord John Russell's speeches in his Parliamentary contest in Devonshire. He accompanied Thomas Beard, who was his companion in the House and his senior on the reporting staff of *The Morning Chronicle*. A letter from Dickens, quoted by Forster, shows how necessary it was to work late into the night, and sometimes all night, in order to despatch the reports, transcribed into longhand, by the earliest possible coaches. He mentions that he hopes to finish the dinner (given that night) in time for Cooper's Co's. coach, leaving the Bush at half-past six

JACK STRAW'S CASTLE, HAMPSTEAD.
A favourite resort,—"a good 'ouse for a red-hot chop."

in the morning. He was then going to Bath to report another long dinner with speeches the same evening, and expected to spend all that night transcribing his report to catch "Ball's First Coach" on Thursday morning. After Bath, he was following Lord John Russell to Marlborough, using the coach journey from Bath to that place for transcribing another speech which evidently was to be made on the day following the Bath dinner. At Marlborough, there would be a further series of speeches, immediately after which it was the intention of Dickens and Beard to return to London by saddle horses.

This brief account gives some idea of the way in which energetic newspaper reporters covered the country in the days before telegraphs were available; it shows something of Dickens's indefatigable character, and it also illustrates enormous quickness of observation and a wonderfully retentive memory in a man who could, during such rushing work, make observation of places (even to small details) for use in books which he wrote in London afterwards. On this reporting trip he stayed at the Bush Inn, Bristol, and, as we are assured by old inhabitants of Bath, at the Saracen's Head, in Broad Street, in the latter city. An interesting little anecdote is told by the landlady of the Saracen's Head, though it can scarcely have belonged to this particular trip, unless Dickens stayed in Bath on his way to Bristol. She tells how the bedrooms of the house were all occupied before Dickens arrived, so that he had to be accommodated in a room over some stables or outbuildings at the farther end of the Inn Yard (overlooking Walcot Street). He sat writing in the house until late at night, when he took a light for his candle from the bar and started across the Yard to his own sleeping place. Just as he reached the foot of the outside stairs leading to his room, a gust of wind blew out the candle, and he returned to the bar for a new light. Carefully shielding it with his hand, he started across the Yard a second time, only to find the light blown out by a gust. Returning, and guarding the new light still more carefully, he again essayed the passage of the Yard; again to find himself in darkness before reaching his destination. The landlady recalled with special satisfaction that although the young gentleman must have started ten or a dozen times and as often turned back to relight his candle, he uttered no single word of impatience or annoyance. At the time of Dickens's visit to Bath, Moses Pickwick & Co. not only ran a series of coaches from London, but also kept the White Hart, a very commodious house for that date, at which Dickens afterwards represents Pickwick as staying. Yet another little association between this reporting trip and *Pickwick* may be found in the fact that one of Dickens's associates at the time was a Vincent Dowling, while one of the characters introduced at Bath is Captain Dowler.

While engaged on newspaper work Dickens was laying a founda-

THE SARACEN'S HEAD, BATH.
Where Dickens stayed on his reporting tour.

tion of magazine articles for a serious literary career, and there are
two little passages in Forster's *Life* and in *Copperfield* which seem
particularly touching. They relate to his first accepted contribution,

JOHNSON'S COURT, FLEET STREET.
With letter-box in which Dickens's first literary contribution was placed.

which he says that he dropped "stealthily one evening at twilight,
with fear and trembling, into a dark letter-box in a dark office up a
dark court in Fleet Street." Of his feeling when he saw his work in
print he says: "I walked down to Westminster Hall, and turned into
it for half-an-hour because my eyes were so dimmed with joy and
pride that they could not bear the street, and were not fit to be seen
there." The "dark court" disappeared in 1902, until which time the
quaint old door and panelled wall and letter-box had remained
untouched. Now they are preserved as mementoes in the offices
built upon the site for Sell's Advertising Agency. The place where
Dickens bought the magazine in which his article appeared, was No.
186, Strand, between Arundel Street and Norfolk Street; a shop long

since pulled down to give place to the great warehouse of W. H. Smith and Sons. Westminster Hall remains, and those who will may stroll therein recalling this incident.

This first work appeared in *The Old Monthly Magazine* in December, 1833, and was entitled "A Dinner at Poplar Walk," afterwards included in *Sketches by Boz*, under the name of "Mr. Minns and his Cousin." During 1834, and the first two months of 1835, some nine further contributions were published by the same journal, all without payment to the author, the first five anonymously, and the others under the signature of "Boz." This name, which will always be wrongly pronounced Bŏz, was a nickname previously given to one of Dickens's younger brothers, who was dubbed Moses, after the character of that name in *The Vicar of Wakefield*, and the title became gradually and nasally corrupted to Boses and Bōz.

The last Boz sketch appeared in the *Monthly* in February of 1835, but as the magazine could not afford to pay anything, Dickens was negotiating with Mr. George Hogarth, his friend of *The Morning Chronicle*, for a series of similar sketches, to run in *The Evening Chronicle*, which was just starting. These were accepted, and his salary, which had been five guineas a week as reporter, was increased by an extra couple of guineas. Through 1835 the sketches were continued, and early in 1836 Dickens collected them for republication in two volumes of *Sketches by Boz*, issued by John Macrone, who was then beginning publishing in St. James's Square, and to whom all rights were sold for £100. Early in the same year two sketches by "Boz," entitled "The Tuggses at Ramsgate," and "A Little Talk about Spring and Sweeps," appeared in *The Library of Fiction*, Vol. I., published by another young firm, Chapman and Hall. Robert Seymour was the artist who illustrated "The Tuggses," and he suggested that he would like to design a series of "cockney" sporting pictures for serial publication. Mr. Chapman thought this might run, if accompanied by letterpress, and the editor of *The Library of Fiction* suggested "Boz" as the likely man. Mr. Hall, the younger partner, called upon the author at his rooms in Furnival's Inn, and Dickens took it as a good augury when he recognised in his visitor

ST. LUKE'S CHURCH, CHELSEA.
Dickens married, April 2nd, 1836.

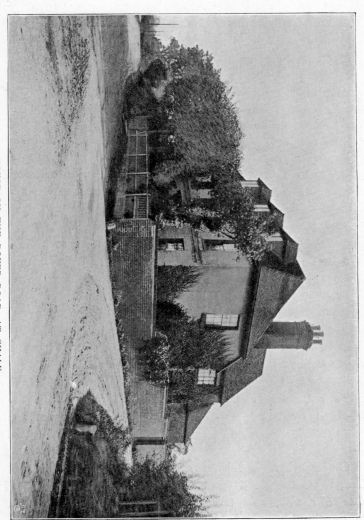

HOUSE ON THE DOVER ROAD, AT CHALK.

Where Dickens spent his honeymoon, and later holidays.

the man who had sold to him, at the shop in the Strand, the number of the *Monthly* containing his first contribution. Arrangements were made for a monthly issue of what Dickens named *The Posthumous Papers of the Pickwick Club*, the payment to be fourteen guineas per issue. Dickens introduced Mr. Winkle in deference to Seymour's ideas on cockney sport, and the proof sheets were submitted to Seymour, who made sketches for two illustrations, depicting Mr. Pickwick as a tall, thin man. Mr. Chapman objected to this, and gave to the artist a description of "a friend of mine at Richmond—a fat old beau who would wear, in spite of the ladies' protests, drab tights and black gaiters."

ST. CLEMENT DANES, STRAND.

The prospectus of *Pickwick* was issued at the end of February, 1836, and on March 31st, the first number was published at one shilling. On April 2nd, Dickens was married, in St. Luke's Church, Chelsea, to Catherine Hogarth, eldest daughter of George Hogarth, of *The Chronicle*, and the honeymoon was spent at Chalk, in a house on the highway between Gravesend and Rochester: on that Dover Road which he introduces so touchingly and tellingly into *Copperfield*, only a few miles from that Gadshill Place which he coveted as a boy and owned as a man, overlooking the estuary of

the Thames and those "meshes" or marshes in which such striking
scenes were laid in *Great Expectations*.

The expense of the honeymoon was met by an advance payment
for two parts of *Pickwick*,
thus showing that Dickens
was far from wealthy; but
during the year appreciation
began to be manifested, he
found some extra occupation
in writing a farce, *The Strange
Gentleman*, and the book of an
opera, *The Village Coquettes*,
both of which were successfully staged, and by the end
of the Parliamentary session
he felt his feet sufficiently to
justify resigning journalism
for literature.

Before leaving this part
of the novelist's life it may
be well to refer to a couple
of evidences of early appreciation which, doubtless,
were most helpful to such a
keenly sensitive man. He tells
in his own letter to Forster,
from which quotation has
been made on this point

GROTESQUES AT CHALK CHURCH.

"Stop to have a greeting with a comical old monk, cross-
legged, with a jovial pot."—Forster's *Life*.

already, that "It was John Black that threw the slipper after me.
Dear old Black. My first hearty out-and-out appreciator." Another
early appreciator of Dickens's works was his Chatham schoolmaster and
friend, William Giles, who sent to him, when *Pickwick* was about half
published, a silver snuff-box inscribed "To the inimitable Boz," a fact
which pleased Dickens so much that in letters to intimate friends he
frequently, and for many years, referred to himself as "the inimitable."

During the latter days of his bachelor life and for some time after marriage, Dickens lived in Furnival's Inn, a great series of buildings on the north side of Holborn, between Leather Lane and Brooke Street, on a site now covered by the buildings of the Prudential Insurance Co. At No. 13, and later at No. 15, in a very tiny suite of three very tiny rooms in each case, he spent many of his happiest days. Removal from the Inn marked his feelings of assured prosperity ; but the old place was always fondly remembered, and was often mentioned in his writings.

TOWN MALLING AND THE SWAN INN.

Suggested by Mr. Charles Dickens, jun., as the originals of Muggleton and The Blue Lion, in *Pickwick*.

Salisbury Cathedral. ("Martin Chuzzlewit.")
(By Catharine Weed Barnes Ward.)

CHAPTER IV

The Writing, and the Scenes of Pickwick

LONDON, ROCHESTER, IPSWICH, BURY, BATH, ETC., 1836—1837

PICKWICK was to be issued in monthly parts, each with four illustrations. On April 20th, 1836, as the second part was in the press, Seymour called upon Dickens in reference to one of the plates, at which time there was nothing in his manner to indicate that (as happened that very evening) he was about to commit suicide. His untimely end came near wrecking the arrangements of the publishers, but they produced the second issue with only three plates, and a sympathetic reference to the artist's death. Before the third number was due, they secured the services of R. W. Buss, a painter and designer, who hesitated to undertake etching, and whose work proved unsatisfactory. The illustrating of the fourth number was placed in the hands of Hablot K. Browne, who adopted the pseudonym of "Phiz" to match "Boz," and this new combination of artist and writer proved permanent and very successful.

LEATHER BOTTLE, COBHAM.

The sale of *Pickwick* began very badly, and much faith was required to continue its issue in the face of disappointing sales and great trouble in securing a suitable illustrator, but both publishers and author had confidence in the ultimate result. Dickens evidently expected Jingle to be very popular, for in a

THE GOSWELL ROAD.

" Goswell Street was at his feet, . . on his right hand, . . on his left, and the opposite side of Goswell Street was over the way."—*Pickwick*.

letter to Catherine Hogarth, before she became his wife, he wrote of the Pickwickians, " They are going on swimmingly in company with a very different character from any I have yet described, but I flatter myself will make a very decided hit." With the fourth number sales began to improve. The fifth (introducing Sam Weller) quickly created a large demand, and by this time another publisher, Richard Bentley, was sufficiently attracted by Dickens's work to make an agreement with him (signed on August 22nd, 1836) under which Dickens was to edit a new monthly magazine, *Bentley's Miscellany*, to be started in the following January.

His growing popularity induced Macrone to decide on re-

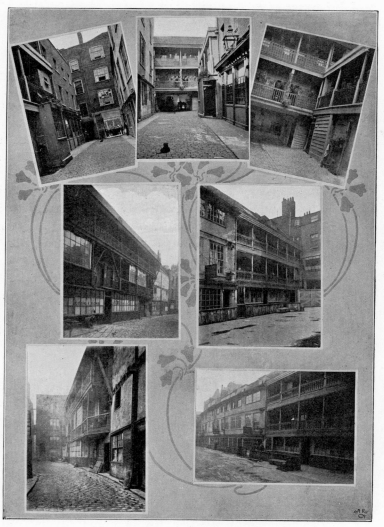

LONDON GALLERIED INNS.

THE BELL.   THE BELL.   THE BELL.
    QUEEN'S HEAD   THE GEORGE.
QUEEN'S HEAD.   THE GEORGE.

E

publishing the *Sketches by Boz* in monthly parts, exactly similar in size and shape to Chapman and Hall's issue of *Pickwick*. This greatly excited Dickens, for he felt that the competition of these less mature papers would affect his reputation in the mind of the public,

48, DOUGHTY STREET.
Dickens's home 1837-1839.

and he therefore endeavoured to induce Macrone to relinquish the copyright, from which he had already made considerable profit. Macrone contended that he had bought all rights and could do as he liked with his own property, wherefore it was eventually felt necessary to buy back what had originally been sold to him for £100, for the very large sum of £2,000. It was then decided to have the *Sketches* issued in serial form by Chapman and Hall, with the result that the profits justified even the large payment made to recover the copyright.

At the beginning of January, 1837, the first issue of *Bentley's Miscellany* was published, and contained the opening scenes of *Oliver Twist*, to which reference will be made in another chapter. On the 6th of January, Dickens's first son (Charles) was born, and about the middle of February Dickens and his wife were again at Chalk, staying in the little house where they had spent their honeymoon. In March, they removed from the small rooms in Furnival's Inn to 48, Doughty Street, a house which still remains, and which is now marked "Dickens House" on the door.

THE BULL INN, ROCHESTER.

"'Do you remain here, sir?' [to Jingle] 'Here—not I—but you'd better—good house—nice beds.'"—*Pickwick.*

E 2

At this time Mary Hogarth, his wife's younger sister, and Fred, his own next younger brother, were living with Dickens, for even in the Furnival's Inn days he commenced that open-hearted hospitality, always beginning with the members of his own family, which remained throughout his life one of his great characteristics. It was a gay, happy, enthusiastic household, working hard, laughing hard, and playing hard; always busy, always restless, and every member enthusiastically bound up in the happiness of all the rest. But a great shock and a great separation were in store for them. On May 7th the whole party had been to some entertainment and returned home in the best of spirits, when, almost as soon as they entered the house, poor Mary Hogarth fell back into Dickens's arms and died almost immediately. The terrible impression made upon him by this loss remained through all his life, and coloured many of his scenes of pathos. We shall refer to it when dealing with Little Nell, and here it is only necessary to say that for very many years Dickens cherished the wish that at his own death he might be laid in the same grave as Mary Hogarth, in Kensal Green Cemetery. Her tombstone bears the simple epitaph written by Dickens: "Young, beautiful, and good, God numbered her among his angels at the early age of 17." The shock was so great that for two months the publication of *Pickwick* was interrupted (while *Oliver Twist* was also delayed), and many curious tales were circulated as to the reason. To the fifteenth issue of *Pickwick* in July, Dickens prefixed a notice explaining the real cause of its late appearance.

Almost immediately after Mary Hogarth's death, Dickens moved for a few weeks to Hampstead, a place whose breezy heights were always very popular with him. Here and at this time began his familiar acquaintance with John Forster, to whom he had been introduced a few months before at the house of Harrison Ainsworth, one of the large number of able and influential men who so quickly gathered around Dickens, and who, to the end of his life, were ever proud of his friendship. Ainsworth and Forster were members of a small party gathered at the invitation of Chapman and Hall for a little dinner early in March, 1837, in honour of the twelfth number of *Pickwick*.

Dickens's restless activity led him to frequently plan walks and rides into the country, to which he would hurriedly invite one or other of his friends.   Hampstead, Highgate, Barnet, Windsor,

THE BULL INN: ENTRANCE AND COACH-YARD.
"The stranger [Jingle] walked briskly up the yard, and turned into the High Street."—*Pickwick*.

Greenwich, Chigwell, and many other places were explored in turn. Jack Straw's Castle at Hampstead was visited at this time, and very frequently afterwards it was the meeting-place of four or five friends to enjoy what Dickens called "a red-hot chop," and to hear him read parts of his manuscript just before sending to the press.

In the beginning of July, Dickens took his wife and "Phiz" for a ten days' holiday on the Continent, where, according to his letter from Calais, they arranged for a post-chaise to take them to "Ghent, Brussels, Antwerp, and a hundred other places that I cannot recollect now, and could not spell if I did."

In August the little family went to Broadstairs, and stayed at No. 12, High Street, where Dickens was for a short time prostrated by illness.

At the beginning of November he first visited Brighton, where he stayed for at least some days, thus showing how fully he was

THE BULL INN : COFFEE ROOM.

Great pleasure—not presume to dictate, but boiled fowl and mushrooms—capital thing ! what time ?"—*Pickwick.*

possessed by a spirit of restlessness, the result of pressure of work, from having undertaken more than he could easily perform. This was very keenly felt about the middle of 1837, for we then find Forster trying to induce Bentley to modify the agreement under which Dickens was bound to quickly complete *Barnaby Rudge,* and also another story, which was to commence in the *Miscellany* immediately after *Oliver Twist.* As a result of these efforts it was arranged that Bentley should abandon his claim to the third novel, and that Dickens should be allowed until November, 1838, to finish *Barnaby.* This would still mean that *Barnaby Rudge* and *Oliver* must be in pre-

paration simultaneously during the twelve months, and that if anything
were prepared to follow *Pickwick* from the hands of Chapman and
Hall there would be no less than three heavy books to be written
simultaneously.

In November, 1837, the last number of *Pickwick* was published, and

THE BULL INN : STAIRCASE TO BALL-ROOM.
"Devil of a mess on the staircase, waiter. Forms going up—carpenters coming down—lamps, glasses, harps.
What's going forward ?"—*Pickwick*.

early in December a dinner was given in honour of the event, when
Dickens took the chair and Sergeant Talfourd was in the vice-chair.
The rest of the party were the publishers (Edward Chapman and
William Hall), John Forster, Harrison Ainsworth, William Jerdan,
and W. C. Macready.

Simultaneously with the publication of the last number, *Pickwick*
was issued in volume form, with the name of the author placed on
the title-page, the first public revelation of the identity of " Boz."   To
Sergeant Talfourd, who had made great efforts in Parliament on

behalf of literary copyright and who remained a firm friend of the novelist until his death in 1845, the volume was inscribed.

Pickwick, the most spontaneous and the most popular of all Dickens's works, is so full of local references that it is impossible to name the whole of them. Yet, wide as is the scope of that remarkable book, it does not cover the whole ground originally intended by Dickens, as we may gather from his announcement published in *The Library of Fiction*, as follows :—

"The Pickwick Club, so renowned in the annals of Huggin Lane and so closely entwined with the thousand interesting associations connected with Lothbury and Cateaton Street, was founded in the year one thousand eight hundred and twenty-two, by Mr. Samuel Pickwick, the great traveller, whose fondness for the useful arts prompted his celebrated journey to Birmingham in the depth of winter; and whose taste for the beauties of nature even led him to penetrate to the very borders of Wales in the height of the summer.

"This remarkable man would appear to have infused a considerable portion of his restless and inquiring spirit into the breasts of other members of the Club, and to have awakened in their minds the same insatiable thirst for travel which so eminently characterised his own. The whole surface of Middlesex, a part of Surrey, a portion of Essex, and several square miles of Kent were in their turns examined and reported on. In a rapid steamer they smoothly navigated the placid Thames; and in an open boat they fearlessly crossed the turbid Medway. . ."

The visit to Wales was abandoned, as well as the scenes in Middlesex and Surrey; for Dickens would never have described London as Middlesex, and Dorking, though it provides some scenes, was not visited by the Club.

Pickwick teems with local allusions. The first chapter refers to Mr. Pickwick's paper, "Speculations on the Source of the Hampstead Ponds, with some Observations on the Theory of Tittlebats," and acknowledges his "unwearied researches" in Hornsey, Highgate, Brixton, and Camberwell. The first speaker in the Pickwickian Debate is referred to as "Mr. Blotton (of Aldgate)." The journey

THE BULL INN : BALL-ROOM.

"A long room, with crimson-covered benches, and wax candles in glass chandeliers. The musicians were securely confined in an elevated den."—*Pickwick.*

of the Pickwickians commenced from Goswell Street (now called Goswell Road), from which Mr. Pickwick walked with his portmanteau in hand to the hackney cab stand at St. Martin's-le-Grand. The whole of this locality has been greatly changed. The

THE BULL INN: BAR ENTRANCE.
"Tickets at the bar, sir; half-a-guinea each, sir."
—*Pickwick*.

Golden Cross, to which Mr. Pickwick was driven, is changed past recognition, although most of the old house still stands behind its modern front. From there, by the coach "Commodore," the friends drove at once to Rochester, the place which was to be intimately associated with so many of Dickens's works, and with the later, as it had been with the boyish part of his life. Strood, Rochester, and Chatham, occurring in this order as approached from London, are really three portions of one town straggling along a single High Street, which is part of the old Roman road to Dover and to Canterbury. The coach would pass the very house where Dickens spent his honeymoon, and it seems rather strange that he makes no reference to any scenes on the road, but takes the travellers direct to Rochester Bridge, from which Mr. Pickwick viewed with admiration and with his pocket telescope the ruins of the Castle. From the same spot a glimpse of the tower of the Cathedral could be obtained, and even in the disjointed sentences of Jingle we find words which, taken in connection with some of Dickens's later writings, show how his earliest observations remained in his memory until his death. Jingle speaks of "Old Cathedral too—earthy smell—pilgrims' feet worn away the old steps—little Saxon doors—con-

fessionals like money takers' boxes at theatres—queer customers
those monks—Popes and Lord Treasurers and all sorts of old fellows
with great red faces and broken noses, turning up every day,—Buff
Jerkins too—matchlocks—Sarcophagus—fine place—old legends too—
strange stories: Capital." In *Edwin Drood* the "old fellows turning

THE BULL INN : COACH-YARD.

up every day" form the subject of Durdles' search for "Old 'uns"
in the crypt of Cloisterham Cathedral; and the earthy smell
remained in Dickens's memory to the latest hours of his conscious
life, for in the last few lines of *Edwin Drood* he writes that
"changes of glorious light from moving boughs, songs of birds, scents
from gardens, woods and fields,—or rather, from the one great garden
of the whole cultivated island in its yielding time,—penetrate into
the Cathedral, subdue its earthy odours, and preach the Resurrection
and the Life."

　　The Pickwickians did not continue the survey of Castle and
Cathedral, but made their way to the Bull Inn, a place so full of

Dickens associations as to be almost sufficient for a chapter itself, and Dickens's interest in this quaint old hostelry becomes very apparent when we remember that it was prominent in *The Great Winglebury Duel*, *The Seven Poor Travellers*, *Great Expectations*, and

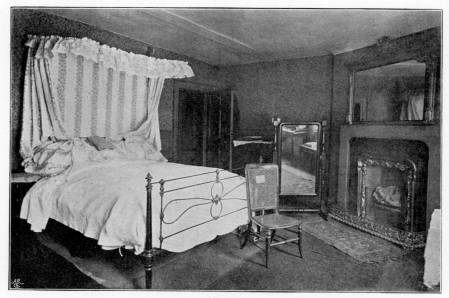

THE BULL INN: PICKWICK'S (AND DICKENS'S) BEDROOM.
" Seven o'clock had hardly ceased striking . . . when Mr. Pickwick's comprehensive mind was aroused . . . by a loud knocking at his chamber door."—*Pickwick*.

Edwin Drood. None of these, however, treated it so humorously or so fully as did *Pickwick*.

The frontage of the house is far from picturesque, and would not for a moment strike the stranger as being likely to inspire humorous or quaint ideas, but when we enter its great archway, under which coaches and post-chaises used to pass to that stable-yard which is now curtailed to a mere fraction of its old-time spaciousness, we realise that we are in one of the curious and comfortable old guest-houses which made so much of the pleasure of travel by high-road. From the roof of the passage hang joints, fowls, and game, awaiting the commands of visitors and the attention of the cook;

and under them to the left we turn through the glass doorway into a square hall, with its staircase zigzagging round three sides of it and reminding us of one of Jingle's early remarks:—"Devil of a mess on the staircase, waiter. Forms going up—carpenters coming down—lamps, glasses, harps. What's going forward?" This was the first introduction to the famous ball, and on the same staircase after the ball Jingle had his altercation with Dr. Slammer, which resulted in a challenge being sent. Immediately to our left is the entrance to the coffee-room where Jingle passed the wine with such effect that Pickwick, Winkle, and Snodgrass fell asleep, while Tupman and Jingle himself made their plans for attending the ball. Here, too, Winkle, to whom Dr. Slammer's cartel was delivered, had his very unpleasant interview with that gentleman's second, and it was through this coffee-room window that Mr. Pickwick's "tall quadruped" showed an inclination to back the post-chaise when starting on the drive to Dingley Dell.

To our right, as we stand in the hall, is the bar at which the tickets for the ball were purchased, while over this bar and the private office and the billiard-room, running back along one side of the stable-yard, is the ball-room itself. "A long room, with crimson-covered benches, and wax candles in glass chandeliers. The musicians were securely confined in an elevated den. . . Two card tables were made up in the adjoining card room, and two pair of old ladies and a corresponding number of stout gentlemen were executing whist therein."

The long ball-room is still used for dinners and festive gatherings, and the "elevated den," with the card room beneath it, remain just as they were in Pickwick's time. Mr. Pickwick's bedroom, No. 17, looks out over the stable-yard, toward the Castle, and is much in demand by visitors (especially Americans); for not only was it the room assigned to Mr. Pickwick, but also the favourite room of Dickens himself on the many occasions when he stayed at the Bull. Its furniture includes two items of Dickensian interest, a cheval glass bought at the sale at Gadshill, and a cane-backed, cane-seated chair which has a curious history. While living at Gadshill, Mr.

Dickens often walked into Rochester with friends, and one of his minor amusements was to turn into a shop where a miscellaneous auction was being held, and to bid for all sorts of things. He usually withdrew from the bidding in time to avoid buying anything but on one occasion this cane chair was knocked down to his bid,

THE BULL INN : TUPMAN'S AND WINKLE'S BEDROOMS.
"Winkle's bedroom is inside mine. . . . I know he has a dress suit in a carpet bag."—*Pickwick*.

when, as he did not need it, he gave a few coppers to a boy to take it to the Bull, with the request that it should be put in Mr. Dickens's bedroom. The bedrooms of Tupman and Winkle are also in demand by visitors, and they communicate, as is stated in *Pickwick*, by an inner door through which Tupman was able to enter Winkle's room although its outer door was locked. The accuracy with which Dickens describes the house shows his wonderful power of observation, and the only slip in the whole description is where he makes Mr. Pickwick speak of Winkle's room as "next door but two, on the right hand," which is hardly a correct

description, since it was on the landing above Mr. Pickwick's. It is
possible that Dickens introduces this mistake purposely, for it will
be seen that although the Boots appeared to have followed Mr.
Pickwick's directions he is said to have knocked at Mr. Tupman's
door instead of Mr. Winkle's.

The scene of the duel was intimately known to Dickens in his
boyhood. The forts are very little changed, so that we may still
"turn into the field which borders the trench, and take the footpath
to the left when you arrive at an angle of the fortification, and keep
straight on . . . to a secluded place."

To compass these Chatham scenes within a walk we may start
along the High Street from Rochester, turn to the right up Star
Hill until a footpath on the left is reached which gives access to
the fields and runs alongside the fortifications. Keeping as nearly
as convenient along the northern side of the fort, the reader will
reach the end of a row of houses with a view of a small public
park and beyond this the roofs of Chatham, with the wide reach of
the Medway and the Government dockyards and forts in the distance.
Looking thus to the north, the rising ground a mile away to the
east of the river is the Chatham "Lines," and No. 11 of the row
of houses behind us (formerly No. 2) is the identical 2, Ordnance
Terrace, in which Dickens lived. Proceeding along Ordnance Terrace
we soon reach the Chatham railway station. Across its front runs
Railway Street, directly continued by Military Road, the main
street of Chatham; near which David Copperfield had the painful
struggle with the old clothes dealer who bought his little jacket.

Just as the Military Road begins to rise towards the naval and
military end of the town, we find on our right the beginning of St.
Mary's Place, along which we must proceed for the sake of seeing
the house in which Dickens lived for a year or two, and the chapel
of Mr. Giles. From St. Mary's Place, going forward by the Military
Road, we soon reach (on the left) St. Mary's Church, and may
continue the same road to the entrance of the Navy Yard in which
still stands the pay-office where John Dickens was employed.
Taking the road up Brompton Hill and bearing round to the right,

AYLESFORD.

Suggested by Mr. Charles Dickens, jun., and accepted by Mr. Hughes, as the place where the Pickwickians crossed the Medway to Dingley Dell.

we come to the "Lines," the wide, open, grassy space where Pickwick and his companions were charged over by the contending forces, and where they made the acquaintance of the genial Mr. Wardle.

When we attempt to identify the excursion of the Pickwickians from Rochester to Dingley Dell the matter becomes a little more

COB TREE HALL, NEAR MAIDSTONE (MANOR FARM, DINGLEY DELL).

"Welcome," said their hospitable host. . . "Welcome, gentlemen, to Manor Farm."—*Pickwick*.

difficult, and there are differences of opinion amongst commentators as to the locality of Muggleton. Mr. Charles Dickens, junior, suggests that Muggleton may have been Town Malling (West Malling), some nine miles from Rochester and about five from Cob Tree Hall, which is generally acknowledged to have been the original of Manor Farm, Dingley Dell. According to *Pickwick*, Dingley Dell was fifteen miles from Rochester, and "not above two miles" from Muggleton. Muggleton itself was a corporate town, with county gaol and sessions house. The direct road from Dingley Dell to London did not lie through Rochester, and altogether, Maidstone and the Cob Tree Hall seem to answer the description given by Dickens far better than any other pair of places; and the identification worked out with great

F

care by Mr. Hammond Hall seems based on irresistible reasoning. The late Mr. W. R. Hughes accepted, with some hesitation, Town Malling as the original of Muggleton, and said that the Pickwickians crossed the Medway by a wooden bridge. Chapter V., however, only says that " the horse dashed the four-wheeled chaise against a wooden

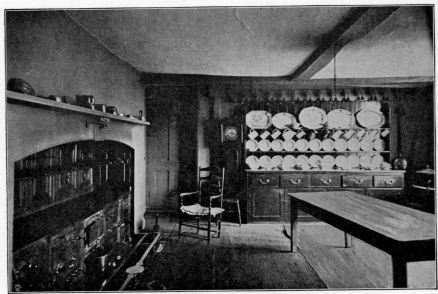

COB TREE HALL (MANOR FARM): THE KITCHEN.

" The large kitchen in which the family were assembled according to annual custom on Christmas Eve.'
—*Pickwick.*

bridge ; " and does not speak of crossing the Medway. Nor can we agree that the description of that accident fits in any way with Mr. Hughes's idea that it occurred at Aylesford Bridge, for in that case there would have been no need of an hour's walking to reach a roadside public-house, for Aylesford itself provided ample accommodation.

Still, Aylesford and Town Malling were places well known to Dickens, and often visited by him on his long walks from Gadshill in later life, so that there is sufficient excuse for introducing pictures of them.

Almost certainly the place depicted as Manor Farm, Dingley Dell, was Cob Tree Hall, Sandling, near Maidstone. Although this house has had additions and alterations since *Pickwick* was written, its front remains much as in Dickens's time, and from its large windows there is a magnificent view over rich undulating country towards

MANOR FARM AND THE FROZEN POND.

"A sharp, smart crack was heard. . . Mr. Pickwick's hat, gloves, and handkerchief were floating on the surface."

—*Pickwick*.

Malling and Rochester, while in the vale below, less than half-a-mile distant, are two large ponds or reservoirs, on one of which Mr. Pickwick had his unfortunate adventure when sliding. Some of the commentators have pointed out that although Cob Tree Hall has no rookery at present, old inhabitants remember a colony of rooks in the trees to the south of the house. The great kitchen, with its one long beam, has a special local interest because it runs along the dividing line between the parishes of Allington and Boxley, and is still quite suitable for the boisterous evening parties which Dickens describes with so much humour. The garden might well provide an arbour in which Mr. Tupman could propose to the spinster aunt and in which they could be interrupted by the Fat Boy ; and Mr. Hammond Hall has shown very striking parallels between the few facts recorded

F 2

of Mr. Wardle's mother and the real facts of Mrs. Spong, the mother of the occupant of Cob Tree Hall in Dickens's time.

The elopement of Jingle with Miss Wardle took Winkle and Mr. Pickwick a tremendous chase across country to London, and to the White Hart in the Borough, a place immortalised by the discovery of Sam Weller, as recorded in Chapter X., which gives incidental reference to Doctors' Commons.

The next chapter takes us back to Dingley Dell, and then, in pursuit of Tracy Tupman who vanished with vague threats of suicide, back to Rochester, possibly by the beautiful and breezy road over Blue Bell Hill and past the ancient cromlech, Kit's Coty House; a road which was greatly favoured by Dickens. Through Rochester and Strood up the London road towards Gadshill, but branching to the left along the old London road (the Pilgrims' Way of Chaucer) before Gadshill is reached, we pass through Cobham Park and part of Shorne Wood, where Mr. Pickwick might very well say, "If this were the place to which all who are troubled with our friend's complaint came, I fancy their old attachment to this world would very soon return." Going forward to Cobham, and entering the Leather Bottle, "a clean and commodious village ale-house," the Pickwickians found Mr. Tupman "looking as unlike a man who had taken his leave of this world as possible," and after encouraging him to finish his dinner, Mr. Pickwick took him to walk in the old churchyard for a little private conversation. After half-an-hour in the churchyard they went down the village, past the Inn, and made a marvellous discovery of the stone inscribed :—

X

B I L S T

U M

P S H I

S.M.

A R K.

a discovery which called forth the suggestion that the inscription had existed "perhaps long before the ancient almshouses in this

THE LEATHER BOTTLE, COBHAM.

" Really, for a misanthrope's choice, this is one of the . . . most desirable places of residence I ever met with."—*Pickwick.*

place." We are glad of this casual mention of the almshouses, for it is the only reference in Dickens's writings, so far as we remember, to a very interesting piece of ancient architecture, formerly a college of priests, and now used for almshouse purposes; a place very familiar to, and much admired by Dickens. The old college buildings

THE LEATHER BOTTLE, COBHAM.

"Entered a long, low-roofed room, . . with a large number of high-backed, leather-cushioned chairs."—*Pickwick*.

adjoin the churchyard, and we may well imagine, although it is not stated, that during the half hour which Pickwick and Tupman spent in their walk, they turned out of the churchyard into the college.

The discovery of this wonderful stone, added to the fact that Mr. Pickwick remembered that the Eatanswill election was just about to take place, determined the party to return to London for a special meeting of the Club, and from there, after the scene in which Mrs. Bardell fainted and Sam Weller was engaged, the whole party started for Eatanswill by the Norwich coach. There can be very little doubt that Ipswich was the place Dickens had in mind when

SHORNE WOOD, COBHAM PARK.

"If this were the place to which all who are troubled with our friend's complaint came, I fancy their old attachment to this world would soon return."—*Pickwick.*

he described Eatanswill, although he specially tells us that Mr.
Pickwick seems to have taken precaution to prevent the place being
identified, and although on the later visit of the Pickwickians, Ipswich

THE GREAT WHITE HORSE, IPSWICH.
" Rendered conspicuous by a stone statue of some rampacious animal . . .
distantly resembling an insane cart-horse."—*Pickwick*.

is mentioned by its
proper name. We
cannot hope to iden-
tify Mr. Pott's house,
at which Pickwick
and Winkle stayed,
or the Peacock,
which accommodated
Tupman, Snodgrass,
and Sam Weller, or
the scene of Mrs.
Leo Hunter's garden
party; but when we
follow Pickwick to
Bury St. Edmund's
we find the Angel
remaining as it was in his time, the principal hotel of the town, with
a spacious stable-yard, in which, if Sam Weller can no longer enjoy
" a half-penny shower-bath " because there is no longer a pump for the
purpose, he may still find " a young gentleman of the stable depart-
ment," and perhaps even a " mulberry-coloured livery," answering to
the redoubtable Job Trotter. The " large old red brick house just
outside the town " where Pickwick had his very unfortunate encounter
with the young ladies' school cannot be identified with any certainty,
for none of the three or four houses confidently pointed out by
different commentators appears to answer the description and to
occupy the required position. It has been suggested, however, that
Eastgate House, Rochester (afterwards described as The Nuns'
House, in *Edwin Drood*), was in Dickens's mind when he depicted
Westgate House, Bury St. Edmund's. If this be so, the description is
not very exact, the only coincidences being the fact that Eastgate
House was a ladies' school and that the names are similar. There

is nothing in *Pickwick* to enable us to identify the land of Sir Geoffrey or One Tree Hill and the adjacent property of Captain Boldwig, where the partridge shooting was followed by Mr. Pickwick's succumbing to the cold punch and his removal to the Pound.

Back again in London, we find a great number of interesting places casually mentioned. Dodson and Fogg's offices were at the end of "Freeman's Court, Cornhill," probably drawn from Newman's Court,

THE ANGEL YARD, BURY ST. EDMUND'S.
"A young fellow in mulberry-coloured livery was sitting on a bench in the yard."—*Pickwick*.

Cornhill, with a name borrowed from a court in neighbouring Cheapside. After the interview with Dodson and Fogg, Mr. Pickwick and Sam crossed opposite the Mansion House, and bent their steps up Cheapside. They turned into the "second court on the right hand side" (Grocers' Hall Court) where the "last house but one on the same side" was a tavern, with a "box as stands in the first fireplace" which was to be preferred "'cos there an't no leg in the middle o' the table, vhich all the others has, and it's wery inconwenient." Here they encountered the elder Weller, with whom they arranged to start back for Ipswich a couple of days later, from "The Bull, in Whitechapel." The far houses on the right hand side have been rebuilt, but Grocers' Hall Court still has its quaint old coffee-houses, including two built around and over the entrance to Dove Court, and dated 1680.

Gray's Inn with its memories of Mr. Perker and Mr. Phunkey still tempts the wanderer.

The Magpie and Stump is said to have stood in Clare

Market, and although the name was borrowed from a house in Fetter Lane, there can be little doubt that the place described was the George the Fourth, or the Old Black Jack in Portsmouth Street (close to the "Old Curiosity Shop" and Lincoln's Inn Fields), which was rebuilt about 1901. This was a district intimately known

ANGEL HILL, BURY ST. EDMUND'S.

"The coach stopped before a large inn situated in a wide, open street, nearly facing the old abbey."—*Pickwick*.

to Dickens, and not far from Clifford's Inn, credited in Jack Bamber's story with being the place where a tenant poisoned himself with a dose of arsenic in the cupboard of his rooms and disturbed his successor by his ghostly presence. Clifford's Inn, alas! at the time of writing, is advertised for sale as a "valuable building site, of nearly one acre."

Jack Bamber's story of "The Queer Client" has its location in the Marshalsea, to which reference has already been made in Chapter II., and which will be more fully treated when we deal with *Little Dorrit*. Another curious reference in the same story, shows Dickens's use of well-known places and place-names, for he is taking us back to the very street where he lived with Mrs. Roylance immediately after his father's days in the Marshalsea, when he writes of going to a "wretched lodging in Camden Town," and of taking a hackney coach to "that corner of the old Pancras Road, at which stands the parish workhouse, . . and, proceeding by the dead wall in front of the Veterinary Hospital, they entered a small by-street, which, whatever it may be now, was in those days a desolate place enough, surrounded by little else than fields and ditches." And of the wife and child of " The Queer Client " he says :— " Beneath a plain grave-stone, in one of the most peaceful

DOVE COURT, LOOKING TO GROCERS' HALL COURT, E.C.
" Second court on the right-hand side—last house but vun."—*Pickwick*.

and secluded churchyards in Kent, where wild flowers mingle with the grass, and the soft landscape around forms the fairest spot in the garden of England, lie the bones of the young mother and her young child." Later, in these pages, many such minor references must be left unnoticed, but it is well to give one or two as showing how, in most casual references, real places, known in his early days, were ever in Dickens's mind.

Before leaving the Clare Market we may remark that in Portugal Street was the Insolvent Court, and "just opposite" was a public-house where Mr. Pell and old Weller met before consigning Sam to the Fleet on his father's affidavit of indebtedness, in order that he might be near his master. To the same house the Wellers repaired after the death of Sam's "mother-in-law," and from it a message was despatched to the Insolvent Court for Mr. Solomon Pell to secure a "probe" of that lady's will.   Both public-house and court have been removed since Dickens's days.

CLIFFORD'S INN.

"Tenant of a top set—bad character—shut himself up, . . and took a dose of arsenic."—*Pickwick*.

The journey from White-chapel to Ipswich has already been referred to in Chapter III. The Great White Horse in Ips-wich still treasures the Dickens associations, maintaining over the door the sign which is much too tame for Dickens's description of "a stone statue of some ram-pacious animal with flowing mane and tail, distantly resembling an insane cart-horse"; and preserv-ing a bedroom in which we are assured that Mr. Pickwick had his strange adventure with the lady in the curl-papers; but it has placed a corrugated iron roof over the coach-yard wherein Mr. Weller, senior, prepared for his return journey to London, and upbraided Sam for his having been "gammoned" by Job Trotter. St. Clement's Church, to which Sam wandered with a view to "dissipate his melancholy," remains without alteration, but the house with "the green gate of a garden at the bottom of the yard," which proved to be the abode of Mr. Nupkins, cannot be identified.

The George and Vulture, in George Yard, Lombard Street, which became Mr. Pickwick's abode after settling his affairs in Ipswich, is so surrounded by mighty modern office buildings that the topo-graphers who have told us it is swept away can scarcely be blamed.

But the old George is still there, and City gentlemen's chops and steaks are still served in the old style.

As for the Marquis of Granby, at Dorking, introduced in Chapters XXVII. and LII., much difference of opinion and of identification exists, while it is difficult to say whether the original of that ancient house either does exist or ever did so. Allbut, an ingenious and

ST. CLEMENT'S CHURCH, IPSWICH.

"Sam . . . endeavoured to dissipate his melancholy by strolling among its ancient precincts."—*Pickwick*.

usually an accurate topographer, identified (1897) a corner grocer's shop in the High Street, opposite the post-office, at the side of Chequers Court, which runs between it and the London and County Bank, as the original; and at least two existing houses make a similar claim or have the claim made for them.

The Christmas visit to Dingley Dell introduces, in the story of Gabriel Grub, "an old abbey town, down in this part of the

THE GEORGE AND VULTURE.

"Very good, old-fashioned and comfortable quarters, to wit, the George and Vulture."—*Pickwick*.

country," which may have been Rochester, or Malling, or even Maidstone, though probably, if any actual place was in mind, it was the more distant Canterbury. Bob Sawyer's reference to his lodgings in Lant Street, where Dickens himself had previously lodged, brings our thoughts back to London, and Chapter XXXI. sees us back at the George and Vulture, takes us up Newgate Street, past the "Celebrated Sassage Factory," into Gray's Inn, and to Lincoln's Inn Old Square, where Dickens spent some months with Mr. Molloy.

Lant Street is the scene of Chapter XXXII.; and we can hear an echo of his own sad days in that dreary region (still partially in its old state) when Dickens says that "If a man wished . . . to place himself beyond the possibility of any inducement to look out of the window he should by all means go to Lant Street." The famous tea-party at Bob Sawyer's was one of the most successful of Dickens's public readings, and one which he thoroughly enjoyed. The reason for Bob's residence in this district was its nearness to Guy's Hospital, about which his student friends told such marvellous stories for Mr. Pickwick's benefit.

There is no Blue Boar, Leadenhall Market, but it has been suggested that the Green Dragon, Bull's Head Passage, Gracechurch Street, was the original of this house, in which Sam Weller wrote his famous "walentine," and where he heard about the meeting of "The Brick Lane Branch of the United Grand Junction Ebenezer Temperance Association," to be held that same evening. Probably few readers of Dickens imagine that the Brick Lane meeting-house had any real existence, but there is to this day, and has been for longer than memory of man reacheth, "a large room pleasantly and airily situated at the top of a safe and commodious ladder," at the back of one of the shops in Brick Lane, where religious meetings are and temperance gatherings may have been held. For this piece of identification we are indebted to Mr. Miller, a Dickensian of wide research, who knows the district thoroughly.

The great trial, Bardell against Pickwick, took place in the Guild-

THE PUMP ROOM, BATH.   EAST END.

"Ornamented with . . . a Tompion clock and a statue of Nash."—*Pickwick*.

hall Court, which is not described in detail, and immediately thereafter Dickens takes us to Bath, a place visited on his reporting tours,
and served by the coaches of Moses Pickwick and Co., from whom
he probably borrowed the name for his first great character. Sam

HOUSE OF ANGELO CYRUS BANTAM, ESQ., M.C.
"Is this 'ere Mr. Bantam's, old feller?"—*Pickwick*.

Weller resents the
fact that "the names
is not only down on
the vaybill, but
they've painted vun
on 'em up, on the
door o' the coach."
The White Horse
Cellar, in Piccadilly,
has vanished as com-
pletely as have Moses
Pickwick's coaches
from the Bath road,
but in Bath itself
most of the Pick-
wickian scenes are unchanged. The White Hart has given way to
the much more pretentious Grand Pump Room Hotel, but the
old sign of the White Hart is still preserved, and is used over
the door of an inn of the same name in Widcombe, a suburb of
Bath.

Two houses in Queen Square have been identified as Mr. Angelo
Bantam's; but we accept No. 12, which is represented in the illustration on this page, firstly because friends in Bath assure us that this
was the residence of the real Master of the Ceremonies, and secondly
because just around the corner is the Beaufort Arms, the principal
meeting-place of the footmen of Bath, and therefore, if it had any
original in reality, the original of the "greengrocer's shop" where
Sam Weller partook of the "friendly swarry, consisting of a boiled
leg of mutton with the usual trimmings."

The Assembly Rooms, with their "ball-room, the long card-room, the octagonal card-room, the staircases, and the passages," still often resound to the merriment of gay and fashionable crowds, and the people of Bath proudly maintain their Dickensian associations. For instance, on Dickens's birthday, 1903, after the unveiling of a tablet on a house where Landor lived and in which "Little Nell" was first suggested to the great novelist, a civic dinner was held in the long card-room, with the Mayor in the chair, distinguished Dickensians from London and other towns amongst the guests, and with a menu limited to foods and drinks mentioned in *Pickwick*, each course marked by a suitable quotation from that work. Permission of the caretaker is needed for viewing these rooms at most times, but the visitor who wishes to see them with any sort of recollection of Mr. Pickwick's impressions should

BEAUFORT ARMS, BATH.

Scene of "a friendly swarry, consisting of a boiled leg of mutton with the usual trimmings."—*Pickwick*.

try to attend some public function, when the lights and the people will do much to help the illusion. He may then amuse himself by selecting modern representatives of Angelo Cyrus Bantam, Esq., Mr. Dowler, the Dowager Lady Snuphanuph, young Lord Mutanhed, Mrs. Colonel Wugsby, Miss Bolo, the Miss Matinters, and the rest. He may even see, "lounging near the doors, and in remote corners, various knots of silly young men, displaying various varieties of puppyism and stupidity; amusing all sensible people near them with their folly and conceit; and happily thinking themselves the objects of general admiration." Or he may observe "the music of

G

soft, tiny footsteps, with now and then a clear merry laugh—low and gentle, but very pleasant to hear in a female voice, whether in Bath or elsewhere"; and note "how brilliant eyes, lighted up with pleasurable expectation, gleamed from every side; and look where you would, some exquisite form glided gracefully through the throng, and was no sooner lost than it was replaced by another as dainty and bewitching." If the modern observer marks these things, and can visualise something of the old Bath from its modern successor, he will realise how facile and how accurate was the man who thus wrote of a place where he had spent but three or four days, and these in the rush of election reporting. For the atmosphere is purely of Bath, not to be confused with that of Cheltenham, or Brighton, or Leamington; and the atmosphere of the Assembly Rooms is quite distinct from that of the great Pump Room, to which the Pickwickians are introduced in Chapter XXXVI.

"The great pump-room is a spacious saloon, ornamented with Corinthian pillars, and a music gallery, and a Tompion clock, and a statue of Nash, and a golden inscription, to which all the water-drinkers should attend, for it appeals to them in the cause of a deserving charity. There is a large bar with a marble vase, out of which the pumper gets the water; and there are a number of yellow-looking tumblers, out of which the company get it; and it is a most edifying and satisfactory sight to behold the perseverance and gravity with which they swallow it. There are baths near at hand, in which a part of the company wash themselves; and a band plays afterwards, to congratulate the remainder on their having done so. There is another pump-room, into which infirm ladies and gentlemen are wheeled, in such an astonishing variety of chairs and chaises, that any adventurous individual who goes in with the regular number of toes, is in imminent danger of coming out without them; and there is a third, into which the quiet people go, for it is less noisy than either. There is an immensity of promenading, on crutches and off, with sticks and without, and a great deal of conversation, and liveliness, and pleasantry." Here is evidence of wonderful observation and wonderful memory. A description written in the rooms could not have been more accurate and would hardly have been so fresh and vivid. Few observers would have noticed that the clock was made by Tompion, or that the statue represented Beau Nash, even if they had seen and

THE ASSEMBLY ROOM, BATH.
"At the appointed hour Mr. Pickwick and his friends repaired to the Assembly Rooms."—*Pickwick.*

remembered that the pillars were Corinthian, and that opposite the clock and statue was a music gallery. The "yellow-looking tumblers," too, yellowed by the saline deposit from the waters, are characteristic of this particular Spa, though not at all an obvious feature to the casual visitor.

With the faculty which he so often showed of selecting at once the salient features of a place, Dickens made play with the hills, and (in the upper part of the city) with the wind. Even the "short fat chairman" and the "long thin one" are said to have been actual

G 2

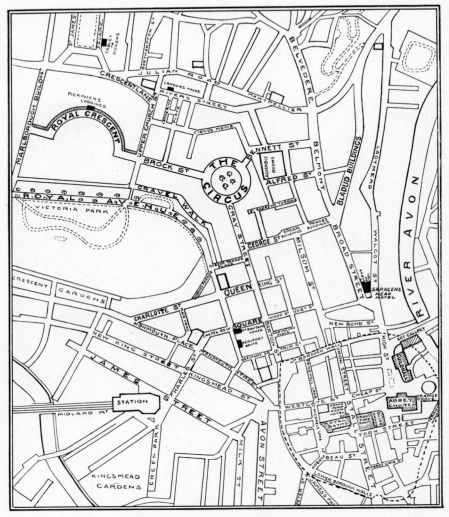

SKETCH PLAN OF THE CITY OF BATH.

well-known characters in Bath in the beginning of last century. They may have been often "blown into the crescent," when, "on that high ground, and in the crescent, which the wind swept round and round as if it were going to tear the paving stones up, its fury was tremendous." The boisterous scene, in which Mr. Winkle was shut out of the house, and almost projected into Mrs. Dowler's sedan chair by the wind, and afterwards chased around the crescent by the infuriated Dowler and the watchman, is a capital piece of

THE GREAT PUMP ROOM, BATH.

"A spacious saloon, ornamented with Corinthian pillars, . . a large bar with a marble vase, out of which the pumper gets the water."—*Pickwick*.

characterisation of locality. Any one who knows Dickens's power in this way will be sure that he really meant the Royal Crescent, and not the Circus, as has often been suggested. The Crescent, opening wide its arms to the south-western gales rushing up from the great broad valley of the Avon, is exactly the proper setting for the incident, which, in the Circus, with its much smaller radius and its tall houses all around, would have seemed forced and exaggerated.

The reason for suggesting that Dickens really meant the Circus lies in the fact that it is said that Winkle "tore round" and that he afterwards "came round the second time." It seems probable that

STATUE OF BLADUD, IN THE BATHS.
"On one of the baths in this city there appeared an inscription in honour of its mighty founder."—*Pickwick*.

Mr. Winkle ran to the end of the Crescent and then below the grass-grown space, along a path which would be the string of the Crescent's bow. The Crescent agrees with the details of the story in a way that the Circus does not, because (as is shown by the rate-books of the time of Dickens's first visit to Bath) while the whole of the houses in the Circus were in private occupation, two, quite at the centre of the Crescent, were lodging houses of the most genteel class. Therefore, while Mr. Dowler and the Pickwickians might readily occupy the upper part of a house in the Crescent, no house in the Circus would be available for this purpose.

We have briefly referred to the scene of the "friendly swarry," which cannot be identified if we are to take Dickens's description of the route of Sam Weller and Mr. John Smauker, who "walked towards the High Street" and later "turned down a bye street" with the reflection from Mr. Smauker that "we shall soon be there."

The flight of Mr. Winkle and the amateur detective exertions of Mr. Weller introduce us to "The Royal Hotel," from which a

branch coach ran to Bristol.   There was no "Royal Hotel" in Bath
in Dickens's time; and his reference is probably to the York House
Hotel, which had been frequently patronised by royalty.   The brief
reference to Mr. Weller's reaching Bristol, "in such time that the

THE ROYAL CRESCENT, BATH.

"Mr. Winkle bounced out of the sedan, . . and, throwing off his slippers into the road, took to his heels and
tore round the Crescent."—*Pickwick*.

pair of horses who went the whole stage and back again twice a
day or more, could reasonably be supposed to arrive there," is
another piece of that careful observation which we find all through
Dickens's works; of the differences between the horses on a small
private or "branch" coach line and those attached to the long
distance royal mail coaches.

    The "Bush," at which Mr. Winkle took up his quarters, still
remains one of the comfortable old hostelries; and some dockside
parts of Bristol may still be described in the few words of Mr.
Winkle "as being a shade more dirty than any place he had ever

seen." Although Bristol and Clifton have an enthusiastic little Dickens Society, and although many people have tried to identify the place "recently converted into something between a shop and a private house" where Bob Sawyer and Ben Allen set up in

THE ROYAL BATH, BATH.
"Baths near at hand in which a part of the company wash themselves ; and a band plays afterwards to congratulate the remainder."—*Pickwick*.

business as medical practitioners this identification seems to be impossible.

It is equally impossible to identify "the stable door at the bottom of a long back lane without a thoroughfare," near which Sam discovered Mary, the pretty housemaid, whom he had last seen at Mr. Nupkins's in Ipswich, and from whom he obtained news of Miss Arabella Allen, and where, later, Mr. Pickwick's dark lantern curiously misled the scientific gentleman.

The opening of Trinity term saw Pickwick back at the George and Vulture, where he was waited upon with an execution by a man from the office of Namby, Bell Alley, Coleman Street, as

BRICK LANE MISSION.
"A large room, pleasantly and airily situated at the top of a safe and commodious ladder."—*Pickwick*.

a result of which he discussed with Perker the relative advantages of the prison of Whitecross Street and the Fleet Prison, both of which have disappeared. On the site of the Fleet Prison, where Mr. Pickwick elected to take his confinement is now the Memorial Hall, Farringdon Street, in which the meetings of the Dickens Fellowship are held. For the obtaining of *Habeas Corpus* Mr. Pickwick was carried off to Chancery

NEWMAN'S COURT ("FREEMAN'S COURT"), CORNHILL.
"In the ground floor front . . . at the furthest end of Freeman's Court, Cornhill, sat the four clerks of Messrs. Dodson and Fogg."—*Pickwick*.

Lane and through the low archway of Serjeant's Inn to where two judges were sitting, after which he was handed over to the tipstaff by whom he was to be conveyed to the Fleet Prison.

We need not dwell upon the scenes in the Fleet, which were undoubtedly drawn from Dickens's experience during his father's monetary difficulties. We have already referred to the Insolvent Court and the public-house opposite, where arrangements were made for the arrest of Sam Weller in order that he might have an excuse for joining his master in confinement, and it is not necessary to deal further with the matter here except to remark that Sam Weller's song of Bold Turpin is still occasionally

TEWKESBURY AND THE HOP-POLE HOTEL.
"At the Hop-pole at Tewkesbury they stopped to dine."—*Pickwick.*

and very successfully sung as a glee, and further, to remind the reader that on the way from the Insolvent Court to the Fleet it was felt necessary to halt at a coffee-house in Serjeant's Inn to refresh the party. The Horn Coffee-House in Doctors' Commons, to which Mr. Pickwick sent from the Fleet Prison for "a bottle or two" which "might be more properly described as a bottle or six" is a recollection of Dickens's days of shorthand-writing to the Proctors, and has disappeared.

The visit of Mr. and Mrs. Raddle and Mrs. Cluppins to the house of Mrs. Bardell takes us back to Goswell Street, and from

THE SPANIARDS. HAMPSTEAD SIDE.

"In a couple of hours they all arrived safely in The Spaniards tea-gardens."—*Pickwick*.

THE SPANIARDS, WITH ENTRANCE TO TEA-GARDENS.

"A hackney-coach at the garden gate. 'Well, if it ain't Mr. Jackson, the young man from Dodson and Fogg's,'
cried Mrs. Bardell."—*Pickwick*.

there we walk with them in quest of the Hampstead stage, by which in a couple of hours they were all safely brought to the Tea-Gardens of The Spaniards at Hampstead. This quaint and not very magnificent old inn, standing opposite the little turnpike gate

THE KITCHEN, SARACEN'S HEAD, TOWCESTER.

"Werry good little dinner, sir, in half-an-hour—pair of fowls, sir, and a weal cutlet ; French beans, 'taturs, tart, and tidiness."—*Pickwick.*

house, still does a large business in supplying teas in the garden for summer-time visitors, and we can only hope that they are seldom so unpleasantly interrupted as were Mrs. Bardell's party when that good lady was arrested by Mr. Jackson, and taken to the Fleet.

The chapter in which Mr. Pickwick's benevolence proved stronger than his obstinacy shows Job Trotter running up Holborn to Gray's Inn, searching for Mr. Perker's laundress, "who occupied the one-pair of some number of some street closely adjoining to some brewery somewhere behind Gray's Inn Lane"; to the Magpie and Stump to find Mr. Lowten; then by cab to Montague Place, Russell Square, to call upon Mr. Perker; finally to Covent Garden Market, to spend the night in a vegetable basket. The chapter finishes with a happy evening party at the George and Vulture, after Mr. Pickwick has bidden adieu to the Fleet Prison.

The next chapter takes us back to Bristol, for the scene in which Ben Allen hears of the marriage of his sister to Mr. Winkle and for the story of the bagman's uncle which was told to the little company at the Bush. This story introduces Edinburgh, with the Canongate, Leith Walk, &c.; and the next chapter, in which Mr. Pickwick starts for Birmingham to see Mr. Winkle, senior, and is unexpectedly reinforced by the erratic Bob Sawyer, takes us through some beautiful country, with a dinner at the Hop-pole Inn at Tewkesbury; and in the gathering

THE ADELPHI.

"She's at Osborne's in the Adelphi at this moment, unless your enterprising friend has run away with her."
—*Pickwick.*

darkness introduces us to the smoky, noisy road close to Birmingham, and later to the Old Royal Hotel, a house which has since been rebuilt.

Chapter LI., taking us back to London, gives a change of horses at Coventry, briefly refers to their changes at Dunchurch and Daventry, and puts down the travellers at the Saracen's Head, Towcester, where, much to their surprise, they find Mr. Pott and Mr. Slurk, the editors of the *Eatanswill Independent* and the *Eatanswill Gazette.*

The chapter which takes us to Dorking and recounts the

discomfiture of Mr. Stiggins makes us regret most sincerely that there is not an undoubted "Marquis of Granby" in its old state, and before it the identical horse trough in which "the shepherd" was half suffocated.

The fifty-fourth chapter takes us to the Adelphi, another district very familiar to Dickens in youth, where old Wardle and Emily make their home when visiting London. The only remaining localities of importance which have not already been dealt with, are Dulwich Church, where the marriage of Mr. Snodgrass was celebrated, the excellent public-house near Shooter's Hill to which Mr. Weller retired, and the new house in Dulwich where Mr. Pickwick peacefully grew old.

TRAFALGAR SQUARE AND ST. MARTIN'S-IN-THE-FIELDS.

"On the steps of the church there was the stooping figure of a man who had put down some burden on the smooth snow. . . . I stood face to face with Mr. Peggotty."—*Copperfield*.

CHAPTER V

"Bentley's Miscellany," "Oliver Twist," and "Nicholas Nickleby"

LONDON, CHERTSEY, YORKSHIRE,
PORTSMOUTH, &c. 1837—1839

OUR last chapter made reference to the agreement to edit *Bentley's Miscellany*, and some of the events of 1837 were briefly sketched. The *Miscellany* was first issued in January, 1837, when Charles Dickens's contribution to its pages was a sketch by Boz, entitled "Public Life of Mr. Tulrumble, once Mayor of Mugfog." In the second number he began *Oliver Twist*, which ran steadily until its conclusion in March, 1839, save for a break in June, 1837, in consequence of the shock of Mary Hogarth's death. The hurry and rush of work led Dickens to undertake for Bentley more than he could possibly perform, with the result that the agreement had to be modified, the writing of *Barnaby Rudge* postponed, and a third novel, which was included in the arrangement, dropped altogether.

WHITE HART, BATH.

On March 6th, 1838, a daughter (Mary, or "Mamie") was born, and on April 2nd a little party dined at the Star and Garter, Richmond, in honour of the anniversary of Dickens's wedding and John Forster's birthday. The early summer was spent in a cottage at Twickenham, and July was marked by Dickens's election to membership of the Athenæum Club, which remained his favourite club-house until his death.   August and September were spent at Broadstairs ; and at the end of October there was a hurried journey

THE ROYAL SURREY THEATRE.
" Oliver Twist " staged November 19, 1838.
Here Fanny Dorrit danced, and her uncle played the clarionet.

with Hablot K. Browne to Warwick, Stratford-on-Avon, Kenilworth, Birmingham, Wolverhampton, Shrewsbury, and North Wales, the results of which are to be seen in the wanderings of Little Nell.

This journey is also incidentally mentioned in *Nicholas Nickleby*,

where Mrs. Nickleby says, with characteristic discursiveness :—" Soon after I was married, I went to Stratford with my poor dear Mr. Nickleby, in a post-chaise from Birmingham—was it a post-chaise, though ! yes, it must have been a post-chaise, because I recollect remarking at the time that the driver had a green shade over his left eye ;—in a post-chaise from Birmingham,"—and so forth.

On November 19th a dramatised version of *Oliver Twist* was produced at the Royal Surrey Theatre ; and on the same evening a pirated version of *Nicholas Nickleby* was staged at the Adelphi. Dickens saw the former piece, and was so disappointed and annoyed that " in the middle of the first scene he laid himself down upon the floor in a corner of the box, and never rose from it until the drop-scene fell."

In February, 1839, there was a famous birthday dinner with

Leigh Hunt, Harrison Ainsworth, and Forster amongst the guests; and in the same month the editorship of *Bentley's* was handed over to Ainsworth, though Dickens's name continued to be associated with it, and so valuable had that name become that for its use alone he received a payment of £40 monthly, exactly double the sum for which he had been glad to undertake the work of editorship less than three years before.

In March, Dickens made a brief visit to Exeter, and secured for his parents' use Mile End Cottage, Alphington, just a mile from the city.

MILE END COTTAGE, ALPHINGTON.
" Tell my father I think it would be a great thing for him to have Dash, if it be only to keep down the trampers and beggars."—Dickens's *Letters*.

At the end of April he took Elm Cottage, Petersham, as a summer residence for himself; and June saw the completion of *Sketches by Boz* in monthly parts (Chapman and Hall) and its publication in volume form. In September, Broadstairs was again visited. Messrs. Chapman and Hall dined with their successful young author to consult him about the illustrations of *Nickleby;* and that book was completed early in October, a fact marked by a dinner at the Albion, Aldersgate Street, with Macready, Maclise, Sir David Wilkie, R.A., Serjeant Talfourd, and Forster amongst the guests.

At the end of October, 1839, Dickens's second daughter (Kate Macready; now Mrs. Perugini) was born, and at the close of the year the family moved from Doughty Street to No. 1, Devonshire Terrace. It only remains to be said of this period (1837–39) that Dickens was enormously busy. Apart from the heavy work of

H

completing *Pickwick*, editing *Bentley's*, and writing *Oliver* and *Nickleby*, he edited the *Life of Grimaldi*, wrote *Is she his Wife?* and *The Lamplighter's Story* for the stage, and produced a great number of minor writings. His ambition is shown by joining the Athenæum, and by being entered as a member of the Middle Temple.

Rejoicing in the success of *Boz* and *Pickwick*, Dickens did not fail to realise that power involves responsibility; and in approaching the first book which was really planned (for *Pickwick* was without plan) he set himself the task of tackling an abuse. That this was in the lines of his natural taste is shown by the treatment of public abuses in some of the minor writings, and by the terrible scenes, whose pathos is often lost in their humour, in the Fleet Prison. In designing *Oliver Twist* he deliberately chose that gang of thieves with their surroundings for the artistic purpose of showing "in little Oliver the principle of good surviving through every adverse circumstance, and triumphing at last"; and for another reason, of which he says: "I had read of thieves by scores—seductive fellows (amiable for the most part), faultless in dress, plump in pocket, choice in horse-flesh, bold in bearing, fortunate in gallantry, great at a song, a bottle, a pack of cards, or dice-box, and fit companions for the bravest; but I had never met (except in Hogarth) with the miserable reality. It appeared to me that to draw a knot of such associates in crime as really do exist . . . would be to attempt something which was greatly needed, and which would be a service to society. And therefore I did it as I best could." Here is the touch of high aspiration, combined with modest appraisement of his own performance, which was characteristic of Dickens all through. His success was based upon the fact that his immense energy, ability, and versatility never blinded him to the need for hard detailed work; and that: "whatever I have tried to do in life, I have tried with all my heart to do well. What I have devoted myself to, I have devoted myself to completely. Never to put one hand to anything on which I could not throw my whole self, and never to affect depreciation of my own work, whatever it was, I find now to have been my golden rules."

NO. I, DEVONSHIRE TERRACE.

"He cared most for Devonshire Terrace, perhaps for the bit of ground attached to it."—Forster's *Life*.

H 2

Perhaps it was well that, in attacking a pauperising system as extensive as the country, the writer should not too exactly identify any one place, lest the others should hug the idea that they were different.   We cannot identify the workhouse where Oliver was born, and the town from which he escaped to London, although the writer seems to give us very careful clues :—

HATTON YARD: BACK ENTRANCE TO MR. FANG'S COURT.
BY MR. T. W. TYRRELL.
" He was led beneath a low archway, and up a dirty court."—*Oliver Twist.*

The town was on or near a canal, because Mr. Sowerberry says (Chap. IV.) that " all the iron handles come, by canal, from Birmingham." The road rose sharply, for Oliver remembered (Chap. VII.) the waggons toiling up the hill. The distance to London was seventy-five or eighty miles, for by eight o'clock Oliver was " nearly five miles away," then " he ran, and hid behind the hedges, by turns, till noon," when he sat down beside a milestone which " bore the intimation that it was just seventy miles from that spot to London." It was on a stage-coach road (Chap. VIII.), which led to Barnet. Towns at about the right distance and in the right direction are Peterborough, Market Harborough, Kettering, Leicester, Rugby, and Coventry.

The little town of High Barnet straggles along the high road without material alteration, save in its suburbs ; but the Fagin district, including Great and Little Saffron Hill, and Field Lane, " near" which was the old Jew's den, is very much altered. Most of the old rookeries have given place to warehouse buildings. There is nothing to identify the place near Clerkenwell Green, where the "old cove" was standing at a bookstall, though the part of Farringdon

Road close to Clerkenwell Road is still one of the principal marts for barrow vendors of second-hand books. The "very notorious metropolitan police office" where "Mr. Fang," drawn from a real Mr. Laing, administered injustice, has been wrongly identified more than once, but Mr. Tyrrell seems to have an unassailable case

CLERKENWELL SESSIONS HOUSE.

"And I very much question," added Mr. Bumble, "whether the Clerkenwell Sessions will not find themselves in the wrong box before they have done with me."—*Oliver Twist*.

when he states (on the evidence of law records and directories of the period) that it was the house now known as No. 54, Hatton Garden.

"A neat house in a quiet shady street near Pentonville" was the home of Mr. Brownlow. The recapture of Oliver in Clerkenwell, the crossing of Smithfield Market (quite different from Smithfield of to-day), the striking of eight by a deep church bell (St. Sepulchre's) and the short talk about the prisoners in Newgate, give a whole flood of light on the characters of Sikes, who knew the inside of the prison, and Nancy, who did not. "The other ken" to which Fagin removed for fear of Oliver's "peaching" was "in the neighbourhood of Whitechapel," distant "a full half hour" from Newgate : while

CRAVEN STREET, STRAND.
" As Oliver knew the name of the street in which Mr. Brownlow resided, they were enabled to drive straight there."—*Oliver Twist.*

Bill Sikes's room was in Bethnal Green (Chap. XIX.). The "Clerkinwell Sessions House," close to the crossing of Clerken-well and Farringdon roads, retains its old appearance and use ; and the journey of Oliver and Bill Sikes, to "crack the crib at Chertsey," mentions many objects which are but little changed. Sun Street, Crown Street, Finsbury Square, Chiswell Street, The Barbican, and Long Lane, all retain something of their old character, though the buildings of Smithfield are new. Hosier Lane brought them into Holborn, where they at once saw the clock of St. Andrew's "hard upon seven." The walk past Hyde Park Corner, towards Kensington, the lift in the empty cart through Kensington, Hammersmith, Chiswick, Kew Bridge, Hampton, Sunbury, Shepperton, and Chertsey, covers ground well known to Dickens, and still retaining, in the parts most distant from London, many of its old features.

The "inland village, among green hills and rich woods," to which

Oliver's friends removed him from Chertsey is too vaguely mentioned
to be identified; and vague is the description of "a family hotel in
a quiet but handsome street near Hyde Park" (Chap. XXXIX.)
where Nancy interviewed Rose Maylie, but the same chapter brings

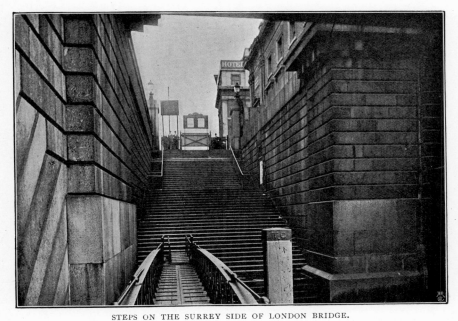

STEPS ON THE SURREY SIDE OF LONDON BRIDGE.

"Not here," said Nancy, "I am afraid to speak to you here. Come away—out of the public road—
down the steps yonder!"—*Oliver Twist.*

up a very definite scene when Nancy promises, "every Sunday night
from eleven until the clock strikes twelve, I will walk on London
Bridge if I am alive." This promise led to that night when Nancy
was followed by Noah Claypole to "the steps which, ... on the
Surrey bank, and on the same side of the bridge as St. Saviour's
Church, form a landing-stairs from the river." The conversation with
Mr. Brownlow and Rose Maylie, overheard by Noah, led to Nancy's
terrible death at the hands of Bill Sikes, as described in a scene
which made the most intensely tragic of Dickens's readings—as we
shall see later. Bill Sikes's erratic flight, through Islington and

Highgate, down Highgate Hill, alongside Caen Wood to Hampstead Heath, to North End, back toward London, a dash to Hendon, then by a spell of steady purpose to Hatfield, a rest in a public-house, and a purposeless tramp toward St. Albans, can easily be followed through the beautiful fields and lanes of which the terrified wanderer took no note. His resolve to return and hide in London, his attempt to drown the wretched, faithful dog, and his journey back to Town by a circuitous route lead up to the scenes at that miserable Jacob's Island of which Dickens says in a preface, " it was publicly declared by an amazing Alderman, that Jacob's Island did not exist, and never had existed. Jacob's Island continues to exist (like an illbred place as it is) in the year one thousand eight hundred and sixty-seven, though improved and much changed." The Island is now entirely improved away, but its site

KING'S HEAD, BARNARD CASTLE.

" There is good ale at the King's Head. Say you know me" (Newman Noggs) " and I am sure they will not charge you for it."—*Nicholas Nickleby*.

may be found about a mile eastward of London Bridge, and a quarter-mile or so from the Tower Bridge, and is bounded by London Street, Mill Street, Jacob Street, and George's Row. Even at time of writing, some of the tenements which replaced those described by Dickens are in parlous state, but only the neighbouring Thames and St. Saviour's Dock remind us of the waterside life of the days when the Folly Ditch (now filled in) took its course along what are now Mill Street, and London Street, and surrounded the Island.

Mr. Brownlow's house, in Craven Street, Strand, mentioned in several chapters, is likely to stand for many years longer, but as we write these words, the pickaxes and crowbars of the house-breakers'

DOTHEBOYS HALL, BOWES.
"A long, cold-looking house, with a few straggling out-buildings behind."—*Nicholas Nickleby.*

men are levelling the walls of Newgate Gaol and removing all traces of those cells in which Fagin spent his last fevered hours.

In November, 1837, an agreement was made with Chapman and Hall, whereby Dickens recovered one-third interest in the copyright of *Pickwick*, and undertook to write *Nicholas Nickleby*, to be issued in twenty parts; the payment to be £150 per part for five years' use of the copyright. The first number appeared in April, 1838; the last two in October, 1839, and the success was very great. Of the first issue some 50,000 copies were immediately sold, and at the close of the volume the publishers gave Dickens £1,500 beyond the agreed amount.

As the Poor Law system had been attacked in *Oliver Twist*, the wretched cruelty of "Yorkshire" schools was exposed in *Nickleby*. For purposes of local colour the author took his illustrator, Hablot K. Browne, to Yorkshire early in 1838, starting by coach on January 30th, from London to Grantham. Next day, from

Grantham to Greta Bridge, where they stayed all night, and on February 1st to Barnard Castle, where the King's Head became their headquarters for a couple of days. On February 2nd they visited some of the schools at Bowes, with letters of introduction

YARD OF DOTHEBOYS HALL.
"Here's a pretty go . . . the pump's froze."—*Nickleby*.

prepared by Mr. Smithson, a solicitor, and in Dickens's note-book is entered: " Shaw, the schoolmaster we saw to-day, is the man in whose school several boys went blind some time since from gross neglect. The case was tried and the verdict went against him. It must have been between 1823 and 1826. Look this up in the newspapers." The neighbours, who knew nothing of this note-book entry, identified Squeers with Shaw, " because he was a schoolmaster, had one eye, and was garrulous."

Certainly he was the man against whom suit was brought, and heavy damages given, in 1823, but his was not by any means the only school of its kind. Reprints of *The Times* have shown that " Mr. Simpson's Academy," Woden Croft Lodge, Yorkshire, near Barnard Castle, was being regularly advertised in 1801 and 1803, while in 1838 (the year of *Nickleby*) the same gentleman advertised from Earby, near Richmond, Yorkshire. " A ruffian named Smith " kept a similar school at Cotherstone, near Barnard Castle, and there were many others. The lawsuit and damages do not seem to have injured Mr. Shaw's reputation, but Dickens's writing had a tremendous effect upon him, and ruined his school, as well as three others in Bowes. A critic described *Nickleby* as " a study in untruth which broke the hearts of two very decent people," and when in Barnard Castle in

1899 we received confirmation of this version from neighbours, intimately connected with the last descendant of Mr. Shaw, who had died but a month or two before. They said that *Nickleby* ruined the school, and broke the nerve of Mr. Shaw, that his daughter

UNICORN INN YARD, BOWES.
Here Dickens called when visiting Mr. Shaw (Squeers).

suffered nervously all her life, and that even her daughter was so much affected that she would only live at Bowes a few weeks in every year, because of her dread of sight-seers. The Bowes people thought sufficiently well of Mr. Shaw to place a stained glass window in the church to his memory; they still maintain that his school was one of the least bad, and that Dickens's attack was more directly against another, and very badly conducted school, at the opposite end of Bowes. A side-light was thrown upon this "least bad" by the driver who took us to photograph the place in 1899, and who had been all through the house a few weeks previously, when the effects were being sold by auction. He said that the garret room, without light and without ventilation, had its ceiling (once whitewashed) covered with candle-smoked names and initials, as far as could be reached by boys standing on their beds; and although he was not a man educated to luxury, the sight of that sleeping room justified, to his mind, all that was written in *Nickleby*.

It has been suggested that the opening scenes of *Nickleby* are drawn from the residence of Dickens's parents at Alphington, but

PRIVATE PARLOUR, KING'S HEAD, BARNARD CASTLE.
Used by Dickens on his visit to the Yorkshire schools.

since the writing was in February, 1838, while the novelist did not take the Alphington cottage until March, 1839, we can scarcely share this view. Golden Square maintains much the same state as in Ralph Nickleby's time, though some of its old houses have given place to new. The house which was identified as Miss La Creevy's in the Strand has been replaced; and the Saracen's Head of to-day is quite as different from the house of Squeers's time, as is Snow Hill from its ancient state ere Holborn Viaduct was made. At the first interview with Squeers he "feigned to be intent upon mending a pen," just as it is recorded that Mr. Shaw did when he granted an audience to Dickens and "Phiz."

Islington, Eton Slocomb, Grantham, and Greta Bridge are briefly sketched from Dickens's own experience, and Newman Noggs's short letter (Chap. VII.) introduces two good public-houses, the Crown, at the corner of James and Silver (now Beak) Streets, close to Golden Square; and the King's Head, Barnard Castle. The house identified as Madame Mantalini's in Wigmore Street, Cavendish Square, has given place to a modern building: the house in Thames Street, where Mrs. Nickleby and Kate were "provided for" as unpaid caretakers, is gone; but a residence allocated to Newman Noggs and the Kenwigs family by Robert Allbut, an industrious commentator, may still be found at 48, Carnaby Street. Manchester Buildings, Westminster, residence of "the great Mr. Gregsbury, M.P.," is gone or going, but Cadogan Place (Mrs. Wititterley's) still "looks down upon Sloane Street, and thinks Brompton low."

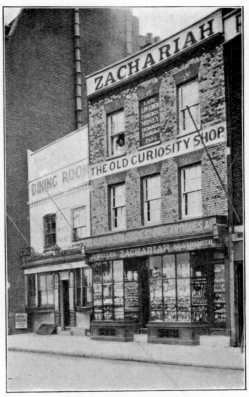

NICKLEBY'S LODGING IN PORTSMOUTH.
"Two small rooms up three pair of stairs . . . at a tobacconist's on the Common Hard."—*Nickleby.*

The country tramp of Nicholas and Smike "to Kingston first," "Godalming some thirty and odd miles from London," along "the rim of the Devil's Punch Bowl," to "the door of a roadside inn, yet twelve miles short of Portsmouth," and the ride into that seaside town with the redoubtable Vincent Crummles, take us through country that is but little changed.

The High Street of Portsmouth retains much of its old aspect, but the theatre disappeared long ago, and for *Nickleby* scenes we are reduced to the view of "the house of one Bulph, a pilot, in Saint Thomas's Street" where Mr. Crummles stayed, and of the "tobacco-

nist's shop, on the Common Hard," where Nicholas found "two small rooms up three pair of stairs, or rather two pair and a ladder."

We should much like to be able to locate the residence of the Cheeryble brothers (portraits of the brothers Grant, whom Dickens visited in 1838 or 1839 at their house in Morley Street), but we can only hesitatingly accept Mr. Percy Fitzgerald's suggestion that it was in "one of the most effective and pic-turesque of City squares—St. Lawrence Pountney Hill." John Browdie's references to the "Poast-office" of St. Martin's-

CARNABY STREET.   HOME OF THE KENWIGS.
"A by-gone, faded, tumble-down street."—*Nickleby*.

le-Grand, which has received a top storey since his day, and to the house "where the Lord Mayor o' Lunnon lives," need no more than a mention here ; and much the same may be said of the dozen or so remaining place-references. There is Canter-bury, where Miss Snevellici felt almost certain she had seen Nicholas ; Ryde, where Mr. and Mrs. Lillyvick went for their honeymoon ; the apartments of Sir Mulberry Hawk and Lord Verisopht, in Regent Street ; Mrs. Nickleby's list of the streets, from Newgate Street to Spigwiffin's Wharf ; the reference to a journey (just previously taken by Dickens himself) to Birmingham and Stratford-on-Avon ; Ralph Nickleby's parcel to "Cross, in Broad

Street"; the handsome hotel "between Park Lane and Bond Street," where Nicholas challenged Sir Mulberry Hawk; the western squares, with which Tim Linkinwater's quiet court where there was a "double-wallflower in the back-attic window at No. 6" was compared; Leadenhall Market, where Tim could buy new-laid eggs; Ralph Nickleby's visits to Pimlico and St. James's Park; the "rules" of King's Bench Prison (now gone), "not many hundred paces distant from the obelisk in St. George's Fields" (soon to disappear); the race-course at Hampton; Eel-pie Island, Twickenham, to which Miss Morleena Kenwigs was invited; the obscure court near Lambeth where Mr. Squeers acted as Ralph Nickleby's aux-iliary; and the labyrinth of streets between Seven Dials and Soho, where Mr. Mantalini's life was "one demd horrid grind." Of these places no more need be said.

THE CROWN, SILVER (NOW BEAK) STREET.
"It is at the corner . . . with a bar door both ways."
—*Nickleby*.

The success of the story has already been mentioned. Its beneficent result was that schools of the class against which it was directed were quickly starved out of existence, because parents and guardians dreaded the shame that would attach to sending their children to such places; and Dickens lived to write of "Yorkshire" schoolmasters in one of his prefaces to the volume:— "I make mention of the race in the past tense. Though it has not yet finally disappeared, it is dwindling daily. A long day's work remains to be done about us in the way of education, Heaven knows; but great improvements and facilities . . . . have been furnished of late years."

SHORNE WOOD, COBHAM.

Dickens's last walk, on Tuesday, June 7th, 1870, was "one of his greatest favourites—through Cobham Park and Wood."—*Letters of Charles Dickens.*

Leicester's Hospital and West Gate, Warwick. (Old Curiosity Shop.)

By Catharine Weed Barnes Ward.

CHAPTER VI

"Master Humphrey's Clock," "The Old Curiosity Shop," and "Barnaby Rudge"

LONDON, THE MIDLANDS, TONG,
CHIGWELL, ETC. 1840—1841

THE Charles Dickens family removed into Devonshire Terrace in December, 1839, and in the new surroundings and larger house the novelist's activities, his lavish hospitality, his measure of success and public recognition rapidly expanded. Regarded at first as a meteoric phenomenon, he now began to be recognised as a power and an authority.

He was greatly troubled with catarrh, more horse exercise was recommended, and Topping, the groom, with Grip, the raven, became mirth-provoking members of the establishment. Early in 1840 he was on the jury charged with investigating the death of a child said to have been murdered by its mother, when, largely through his efforts, the conviction was only for concealment of birth ; and it is a curious coincidence that in an important similar case some fifty years later the eloquence of Henry F. Dickens, the novelist's son, secured the acquittal of a

KING'S HEAD, CHIGWELL.

I

young woman who was found half-starved, half-frozen, with her baby dead and roughly buried in a sand-heap.

At the end of February, Dickens, with his wife, Maclise, and Forster, visited Walter Savage Landor, at 35, St. James's Square, Bath,

THE ALLEGED "OLD CURIOSITY SHOP."

and spent three happy days. While there, he received the suggestion for Little Nell, and met a young girl who furnished some characteristics for that gentle heroine. The house is now marked with a tablet to Charles Dickens. On April 2nd, the wedding-day was celebrated by a dinner at Richmond; on the 3rd, Mr. and Mrs. Dickens went to Birmingham; and on the 4th they were joined by Forster, who reported the magnificent sale of 60,000 copies of the first issue of *Master Humphrey's Clock*, on the day of publication. This was a new, weekly venture, published by Chapman and Hall, who undertook to pay the author £50 an issue for twelve months, whether the venture were successful or not, with a half share of the profits in addition.

In June, 1840, Dickens paid to Bentley the sum of £2,250 for release from his agreement to write *Barnaby*, and for the copyright and stock of *Oliver Twist*. In June and September he made lengthy visits to Broadstairs; and in June ran over to Rochester, Chatham, and Cobham for a couple of days. In August he spent a few days in Devonshire.

In 1841, Dickens edited and revised a series of articles under the title of *Pic Nic Papers*, which were published for the benefit of the widow of Macrone, his first publisher, who had driven such a hard bargain with the young inexperienced author. The *Papers* realised some £300 profit. On February 8th of this year a son was born, and named Walter Landor, and in the same month Dickens ran down to Brighton for a week's quiet work. On March 12th,

VIEW FROM BUTLER'S WHARF (SITE OF QUILP'S) LOOKING DOWN THAMES.

"Quilp very deliberately led the way to the wharf, and reached it between three and four o'clock in the morning."—*Old Curiosity Shop.*

Grip (the first) died, and on the 25th there was a letter inviting Forster to ride to "Chigwell, my dear fellow, the greatest place in the world. Such a delicious old inn opposite the churchyard—such a lovely ride—such beautiful forest scenery—such an out-of-the-way rural place—such a sexton."

In April Dickens was pressed to enter Parliament for Reading, but declined, as being unable to afford the expense. Late in June he started for Scotland, taking work with him. On the 25th there was a great public dinner at Edinburgh, with an enormous ovation, and the days from the 26th to July 3rd were one continuous string of dinners, receptions, &c. From the 4th to the 18th was spent in

I 2

travel through Stirling, Callander, Loch Earn, Killin, Glencoe, Ballachulish, Dalmally, Inverary, Melrose, Abbotsford, and Dryburgh, and it is very surprising, in view of the interesting and enthusiastic letters from this trip, that Scottish scenes were not prominently introduced into any of the works.

SHREWSBURY.

"A number of old houses built of a kind of earth or plaster, crossed and re-crossed in a great many direc- -tions with black beams."—*Old Curiosity Shop*.

August and September saw another long visit to Broad- stairs ; and on the 7th of Sept- ember, as a result of Dickens's dissatisfaction with the weekly form of publication, a new agreement was signed with Chapman and Hall. A visit to America was decided upon, but before sailing there was a visit (in October) to Rochester, and the scenes of boyhood. On October 28th Dickens had the sad duty of attending the funeral of his wife's youngest brother, for which he made the arrange- ments and by whose death he was greatly affected. In Nov- ember *Barnaby Rudge* was fin- ished, and Dickens was ordered to Richmond and Windsor for a few days for the benefit of his health. In December, Landor came from Bath for the christening of the godson who had been born in February; and the house in Devonshire Terrace was let in anticipation of the American trip.

The *Old Curiosity Shop* had no such earnest philanthropic aim as the two previous books, though its tragedy is very touchingly developed from the gambling fever of Little Nell's grandfather. It leads us through some of the loveliest of English landscape, and although its localisation is not absolutely definite it has been possible, by study of the evidence, in connection with Dickens's known journeys in the Midlands, to fit the important points with reasonable certainty. Alfred Rimmer makes the pilgrims wander through the east of London, to Chipping Ongar, where they meet Codlin and

BANBURY (SCENE OF THE RACES), THE REINDEER YARD.

"In the large inn-yards waiters flitted to and fro, and ran against each other, horses clattered on the uneven stones, carriage steps fell rattling down."—*Old Curiosity Shop.*

Short; to Thaxted or Saffron Walden, and thence to Newmarket, for the races. Near Hadleigh, or Ipswich, or Stowmarket, he places the village of the schoolmaster, and finishes by admitting that he cannot find a suitable place for the death of Little Nell. Such an identification ignores the reference (Chap. XV.) to the hill from which St. Paul's might be seen, and "the invading army of bricks and mortar . . . nearly at his feet," forgets that the road to the schoolmaster's village led "downwards in a steep descent" to "the woody hollow below," and it makes no provision for the "black country" part of the journey. Much more satisfactory is the route worked out by Mr. Alfred Watkins, and given in a lecture to the Dickens Fellowship, which ought to be published. He holds that Hampstead Heath is the only possible place for the first rest, and view of St. Paul's. The next stages are uncertain, and the

TONG CHURCH PORCH. BY MR. GEO. E. BROWN.
"Let us wait here," rejoined Nell, "we will sit in the church porch."—*Old Curiosity Shop.*

suggestion is made that the wanderers got on to the Uxbridge Road, the old Worcester coach road, where they met Codlin and Short at some village, — possibly Beaconsfield, High Wycombe or West Wycombe. Islip Bridge and other bridges on the road would fill the requirement that "sometimes they played out the toll across a bridge or ferry," and Banbury, which had a busy race-meeting in Dickens's day, is suggested as the race-town, with the large inn-yards that were so busy. Warmington, a village of some five hundred inhabitants, five miles to the northward of Banbury, answers very well to the description of the schoolmaster's village. Warwick answers in most respects to the town in which Mrs. Jarley showed her wax-works. It has two picturesque town-gates and it has suitable assembly rooms for the exhibition. "Up the steep hill, crowned by the old grey castle," would better apply to Kenilworth than to Warwick, and is probably a reminiscence of the Kenilworth visit. The journey by canal could well be made from Warwick, by the Birmingham and Midland Canal, over part of the route so charmingly described in William Black's *Strange Adventures of a House-boat.* No doubt Birmingham was the place where they left the canal barge, Wolverhampton where the schoolmaster was over-taken, and Shrewsbury the large town with a large church and "a number of old houses, built of a kind of earth or plaster, crossed and re-crossed in a great many directions with black beams, which gave them a remarkable and very ancient look." These places agree well with the distances and description, and they all were included

TONG CHURCH. BY MR. W. W. NAUNTON.

" Under the porch where she had sat when Heaven in its mercy brought her to that peaceful spot, she passed again, and the old church received her in its quiet shade."— *Old Curiosity Shop.*

in Dickens's journey with "Phiz." Of the village where Little Nell died, Tong, with its beautiful old church, formed the original. Its position is too near Wolverhampton to fit the story of the long waggon journey, and to reach it by way of Shrewsbury would be going twice over almost the same ground, but Tong was the place sketched by Cattermole, and it fits Dickens's description, even to minute and incidental details.

The affecting story of Little Nell's death need not be described here, but its effect upon the writer may be briefly stated in his own words, quoted from two letters to Forster :—" All night I have been pursued by the child, and this morning I am unrefreshed and miserable. I don't know what to do with myself." Later, "Nobody will miss her like I shall. It is such a very painful thing to me that I really cannot express my sorrow. Old wounds bleed afresh when I only think of the way of doing it ; what the actual doing it will be, God knows." The effect upon others was equally great, for men of high intellectual attainment implored, as the catastrophe became imminent, that the child should not be allowed to die.

Few scenes other than those of the journey remain and are identifiable. The old curiosity shop itself cannot be connected with the one at the corner of Lincoln's Inn Fields which has been visited by so many thousands of pious pilgrims from all parts of the world ; for Allbut states that Dickens himself pointed out No. 10, Green Street, Leicester Square (a shop long since rebuilt) as the actual original. Covent Garden remains, as so wonderfully described, Quilp's home on Tower Hill has disappeared, and his wharf is now covered by the great warehouse buildings of Butler's Wharf, close to the eastern side of the southern end of the Tower Bridge. At the east end of the wharf a public landing-stairs leads down to the river, and gives such a view of the Thames and shipping as Quilp's would have given us had it remained. The Tower of London, mentioned in this and other books, still well rewards the visitor, and is illustrated in a later chapter. Drury Lane may be searched in vain for Dick Swiveller's apartments, for improvement has swept away the rookery portion ; and the old houses in Bevis Marks where Dickens went to see that there was a suitable home for Sampson Brass, are gone.

Abel Cottage, Finchley, may have been any one of several old cottages still lingering beside the Great North Road, and there are still many places in Whitechapel where Sally Brass, "a rare fellow for a bargain" might find a second-hand stool for Dick Swiveller. Astley's Theatre still graces the Westminster Bridge Road, though its name and status have more than once changed. The Mansion

THE KING'S HEAD ("MAYPOLE"), CHIGWELL.

"Such a delicious old inn opposite the churchyard."—*Dickens's letter to Forster.*

THE "CHESTER" ROOM AT THE KING'S HEAD.

"Mr. Chester . . . signified that he wanted a large apartment. . . 'Why, then, I'll tell you what : . . . he
and Mr. Haredale are going to fight a duel in it.'"—*Barnaby Rudge.*

House, connected with Kit's arrest, remains, but the Old Bailey (or Newgate) is rebuilding.

Barnaby Rudge is supposed to have its opening scenes laid in the King's Head, Chigwell, that "delicious old inn opposite the church-

64, WELBECK STREET.
House of Lord George Gordon.

yard" to which reference has already been made. And this is maintained in spite of the fact that there is a "Maypole" Inn at Chigwell Green, some two miles away. The King's Head is a picturesque old house, though not at all in the archi-tectural style of the Maypole used in illustration of *Barnaby*, and it has a magnificent old upstairs room suitable for the discussion between Chester and Haredale, and between Lord George Gordon and his secret-ary Gashford. Gabriel Varden's house in Clerkenwell cannot be identified, nor can the cellars, off the Barbican, where Sim Tap-pertit met his 'Prentice Knights. "By-streets in Southwark, not far from London Bridge," still contain houses that were stand-ing in Dickens's time and that would pass for the lodgings of Mrs. Rudge, but there are not sufficient indications in the book to identify a house, or even the street. Temple Bar, disliked by the 'prentices because it was "strictly constitutional," is now at Theobalds, near Waltham. The Warren, at Chigwell, cannot be found, which is quite in keeping with Dickens's statement that it was burned down. The Black Lion in Whitechapel we may not find, but the Monument remains, where

ST. JOHN'S GATE, CLERKENWELL.

Joe Willet was advised to spend his time, and sixpence, because "there is no temptation there, sir — no drink — no young women — no bad characters of any sort — nothing but imagination."

THE SARDINIA ARCHES.
"The men who are loitering in the streets to-night are half disposed to pull down a Romish chapel or two."—*Barnaby*.

The Temple — Paper Buildings, in King's Bench Walk —still has many suites suitable for the rooms of Mr. Chester, and one of these is occupied by Mr. Henry F. Dickens, K.C., the son of the novelist.

The fine description of London streets in the end of the eighteenth century, which comes at the beginning of Chapter XVI.,

CHAIR AND COPPER POT FROM THE KING'S HEAD.
"Mr. Willet sat with his eyes on the eternal boiler."—*Barnaby*.

is well worthy of Dickens, and gives a characteristic setting for the uncouth and fierce elder Rudge; but we need not follow him through all his aimless wanderings between Cornhill and Smithfield, even though they do bring us to a mention of that City gaol (Newgate) which is to loom so large in the story.

The noted coffee-house in Covent Garden (Chapter XXVIII.) was, doubtless, Cuttriss's, where Dickens often visited, and Joe Willet's melancholy walk by Islington to Highgate, before enlisting for "the Salwanners" can easily be followed. No. 64, Welbeck Street, still stands, though the separate balcony from which Lord George Gordon addressed the mob, has been replaced by a continuous one in front of more than one of the windows; but if we follow that ragged procession from Whitechapel, through Leadenhall Street, Cheapside, St. Paul's Churchyard, the Strand, and Oxford Street to Welbeck Street, we pass through streets almost entirely altered since the time of which *Barnaby* treats. A modern "Boot" stands in one of the streets behind the Foundling Hospital, on the site of the old Boot Tavern where the rioters met. St. Dunstan's, Fleet Street, whose "giants struck the hour above" Maypole Hugh, is still a beautiful object: though its pump, at which he became "almost sobered for the time," has now no better representative than a marble drinking fountain. Westminster Hall, meeting-place of Gashford, Sir John Chester, and Mr. Haredale, is still open to the public.

LEATHER LANE.

"Barnaby sprang up behind him, snatched the bridle, turned into Leather Lane."—*Barnaby Rudge.*

The "small English county town, the inhabitants of which supported themselves by the labour of their hands in plaiting and preparing straw for those who made bonnets," and where Barnaby and Mrs. Rudge dwelt quietly for five years must have been Luton, though the time spent in wandering from there to London seems unnecessarily long. The streets through which the rioters marched, from their meeting in St. George's Fields, over the various bridges to the House of Commons; the streets and squares which rang with their orgies and plunder and destruction; the scenes at the Sardinia Chapel, at Lord Mansfield's house, at

Newgate, and at Tyburn; the frightened hiding in the lanes and fields or the terrible scenes at the gallows, need no description here. The Sardinia Chapel still remains, though doomed and presenting no picturesque features to the street. The Tower, to which Lord George was confined, still frowns in its ancient strength, and though Newgate is gone, the dread bell of St. Sepulchre's, which has tolled so many knells of living men, still hangs in its belfry. The burning of a part of Newgate was a historical fact, and at the recent sale of portions of the material of that prison there were beams and door-jambs charred by the rioters.

The house of Langdale, the vintner, which offered insecure asylum to Mr. Haredale, remained unchanged at the corner of Holborn and Fetter Lane until about 1900; and there is still some of the old quaintness about Leather Lane, along which the rioters surged to the attack of that house, although the picturesque overhanging houses that almost met at the Holborn end are gone. Lincoln's Inn Fields, a well-kept County Council public garden, bears no resemblance to the Fields of the time of the riots; and much the same may be said of Bloomsbury Square, where Barnaby had such a narrow escape from hanging, although that square is now, as it was then, private property.

This chapter must close with the mention of a few of the casual place-references of small importance. "Golden Lion Court, number twenty-sevin, second bell-handle on the right-hand door-post," is mentioned as the residence of a married sister of Miss Miggs, in Chapter XLI. and again in LXX. The famous Chelsea Bun-house is visited by the Royal East London Volunteers (Chapter XLII.), a trip from the Tower Stairs to Gravesend by the tide boat, and thence overland to Canterbury, is recommended for the safety of Sim Tappertit (Chapter LI.), and even Bristol and its coach-office receive casual mention in the last chapter but one.

THE HORSE GUARDS.

" At this crisis Mark Tapley interposed with an apology for remarking that the clock at the Horse Guards was striking."—*Chuzzlewit*.

CHAPTER VII

First American Tour, " American Notes," and " Martin Chuzzlewit "

THE " BRITANNIA," THE UNITED STATES, SALISBURY, AMESBURY, LONDON, ETC. 1842—1844.

THE SPANIARDS.

HAPMAN AND HALL made a very generous agreement for the publication of the first novel after the American tour. It was to be begun in November, 1842, after giving the writer twelve clear months for rest and travel, and was to be paid for at the rate of £200 per month, irrespective of success, plus three-quarters of the profits in case of success. Meanwhile, for each of the twelve idle months £150 was to be paid, as an advance in respect of profits beyond the £200 per monthly number; for the monthly form of publication was to be resumed. This advance, added to a steady income from the earlier books, enabled Dickens to take the American tour, on which his heart was set, without financial difficulty.

On January 1st, 1842, there was a little dinner of farewell to English friends, and on January 2nd Mr. and Mrs. Dickens went to

THE "BRITANNIA" (CUNARDER).
In which Dickens crossed to America, 1842.
By permission of Messrs. Ridley and Co.

Liverpool, where they stayed at the Adelphi Hotel until the day of sailing, the 4th. The *Britannia* (Cunarder) had a most tempestuous passage, and ran aground in Boston Harbour, but eventually landed everyone safely. At a meeting of the passengers on January 21st, the Earl of Mulgrave was voted to the chair, and Dickens was made secretary and treasurer of a scheme to present a piece of plate to Captain Hewett in acknowledgment of his skill and seamanship.

The early part of the American trip was rendered most enjoyable by the enthusiasm and hospitality of friends and admirers, but friction soon arose from Dickens's strong and very frank utterances in favour

"CHUZZLEWIT" SCENES AT AMESBURY.

THE GEORGE (BLUE DRAGON).   GEORGE YARD.
THE TOLL-BAR HOUSE   PECKSNIFF'S HOUSE.
OLD CHUZZLEWIT'S BED-ROOM.   AMESBURY CHURCH.

K

of international copyright ; and later he was much troubled by the
signs of slavery, to the south, and by the rude offensive habits of
some of the people in what was then considered the far west.
The party arrived in Boston on January 21st, and had a busy fort-

THE GEORGE INN (BLUE DRAGON), AMESBURY.
" Nearly the whole family sat down before the Blue Dragon and formally invested it."—*Chuzzlewit.*

night of theatres, balls, receptions, public and private dinners, and
visits to prisons, asylums, workhouses, &c.

At Worcester, Springfield, Hartford, New Haven, and New York
they were enthusiastically received and lavishly entertained.   One of
the most important of these functions, from Dickens's own point of
view, was a breakfast with Dr. Channing on February 2nd.

On March 5th they left New York, where Dickens had been
detained by severe catarrh.   On the 13th they were at Washington,
on the 15th attended a *levée* at the house of the President, on the
16th left for Richmond, Virginia, and on the 20th they were back
again in Washington.   The 21st to the 24th were spent in Baltimore,

where Washington Irving dined with Dickens. The Western trip began on the 24th, by train to York, thence by coach to Harrisburg, where a canal-boat was taken as far as Pittsburg (reached on the 28th). A Mississippi steamer carried them forward, and aboard that boat they held a feeble imitation of the annual wedding-day celebration on April 2nd. The 4th

HIGH STREET, SALISBURY.

Tom Pinch "took leave of his friend, . . . groped his way out into the now lamp-lighted streets, and hurried off to his dinner."—*Chuzzlewit*.

and 5th were spent in Cincinnati ; on the 6th a mail boat took them to Louisville, and on the 7th they went forward by another steamer for St. Louis, which was reached on the 10th. A day of sight-seeing in the city, a day and a half of driving to see a sun-set on the prairie, followed by a soiree and ball, filled the time in St. Louis ; the 17th saw them back at Louisville,

SALISBURY : THE POULTRY CROSS.

Visited by Tom Pinch on market day, when "the thoroughfares about the market-place were filled with carts, horses, donkeys, baskets, waggons, . . . tripe, pies, poultry, and hucksters' wares of every description."—*Chuzzlewit*.

and the 19th at Cincinnati, whence they travelled by coach all night to Columbus, Ohio. Columbus was reached at 7 a.m., sleep was taken until noon, when they were "at home" to the townsfolk for a couple of hours; went sight-seeing, and attended a reception in their honour in the evening. Columbus to Sandusky by private coach was a drive of two days over terrible roads; thence a steamer took

PUMP COURT, TEMPLE.
"There was a ghostly air . . . attending every circumstance of Tom's employment there, which had a strange charm."—*Chuzzlewit.*

them forward to Buffalo, tying up for the night at Cleveland, Ohio. On April 6th Buffalo was reached, and a very short train run took them to Niagara, whence Dickens wrote an enthusiastic letter on May 1st, and in *American Notes* he writes in retrospect: "I think in every quiet season now, still do those waters roll and leap, and roar and tumble, all day long; still are the rainbows spanning them a hundred feet below. Still, when the sun is on them, do they shine and glow like molten gold. Still, when the day is gloomy, do they fall like snow or seem to crumble away like the front of a great chalk cliff, or roll down the rock like dense white smoke. But always does the mighty stream appear to die as it comes down, and always from its unfathomable grave arises that tremendous ghost of spray and mist which is never laid; which has haunted this place with the same dread solemnity since Darkness brooded on the deep, and that first flood before the Deluge— Light—came rushing on Creation at the word of God."

The whole of May was spent in Canada, with some most successful private theatricals in Montreal; and early in June Dickens was home again, when a small "welcome home" dinner was given at Greenwich. About the end of June the annual visit to Broadstairs began; and about this time, too, Miss Georgina Hogarth, sister of Mrs. Dickens, became a member of the family, and remained so until after the novelist's death.

American Notes was finished in October, at which time Longfellow was Dickens's guest, and with him visited Rochester Castle and spent a night amongst the thieves' dens of London. Longfellow sailed for home from Bristol on October 21st, and immediately thereafter Dickens visited Cornwall with Stanfield, Maclise, and Forster, for he intended to open *Martin Chuzzlewit* with scenes in a lighthouse and on the Cornish coast.

While in America, Dickens became much interested in

SALISBURY CATHEDRAL.

"Now, the organist's assistant was a friend of Mr. Pinch's, so while he played, Tom helped him with the stops."—*Chuzzlewit.*

Unitarian thought, through meeting some of the ablest Unitarians, and on return to London began to attend the Essex Chapel (now Essex Hall) in Essex Street, Strand. There he saw an announcement of a sermon on Dr. Channing (just deceased) to be given at Little Portland Street Chapel, on November 20th. This he attended, and

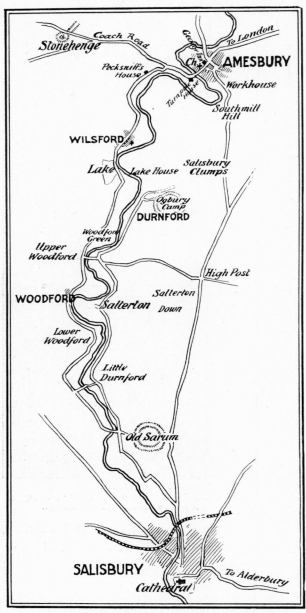

PLAN OF THE SALISBURY-AMESBURY DISTRICT.   Scale ½ inch to a mile.

so much appreciated the sermon that he became a seat-holder at Little Portland Street, a useful, active member of the congregation, and a firm friend of the Rev. Edward Tagart, the pastor.

The first number of *Martin Chuzzlewit* was produced in December, 1842, dated January, 1843. In February, 1843, overworked and indisposed, a rest at Richmond was needed, and immediately afterward a cottage at Finchley was taken. The wedding anniversary was spent at Richmond, as usual, and in July Dickens had a short visit in Yorkshire as the guest of Mr. Smithson, who had introduced him to the "Yorkshire schools."

In July there was a rupture with Chapman and Hall, resulting, apparently, from ultra-sensitiveness on Dickens's part, and he made a publishing agreement (to which we shall refer in the next chapter) with Bradbury and Evans. Autumn saw the usual Broadstairs visit; in October Dickens presided over a soiree at the opening of the Manchester Athenæum; and in November, wearied and worried, he proposed to retire from work for one year.

With the *Christmas Carol*, published in December, 1843, the next chapter will

THE MONUMENT.

"With every hair erect upon his golden head as if the doings of the city frightened him."—*Chuzzlewit*.

deal, and here it only remains to say that Dickens was greatly in demand during the year as a president and speaker at dinners, charitable meetings, and literary functions.

It is not our purpose to deal with the scenes of *American Notes* nor with the American scenes of *Chuzzlewit*, although when we were lecturing in Louisville in 1899 the elevator "boy" at the

KING'S HEAD COURT.

"Mr. Pecksniff was . . . conducted to her peaceful home beneath the shadow of the Monument, by Mrs. Todgers."—*Chuzzlewit*.

hotel told us that he had read the book three times, and volunteered the information that he "knew Cairo very well—just down here y'know—place Dickens called Eden—just like Eden to this day—land sharks, lots of 'em."

There are people who suggest that Alderbury, a short three miles south east of Salisbury, is the place of Mr. Pecksniff's practice, sim-

BELL INN AND BLACK BULL, HOLBORN.   BY MR. A. E. WADE.
" I'm glad to see a parapidge in case of fire, and lots of roofs and chimley-pots to walk upon."—*Chuzzlewit.*

BLACK BULL CHAMBERS.
"As she turned into the yard, she stopped, for the landlord, landlady, and head chambermaid were all on the threshold together, talking earnestly."—*Chuzzlewit.*

ply because that village has a dragon of some colour for the sign of one of its inns. But anyone who really studies the story of Chuzzlewit, with ordnance map before him and a knowledge of the old coach routes, will find that Amesbury, some eight miles to the north of Salisbury, answers in every detail save that its church is described as having a spire (really it has a square tower), just as Dickens talks of the towers of Salisbury Cathedral coming into view, although he well knew that its single tall taper spire is its great characteristic. Though Amesbury has no Blue Dragon, it has a George

Inn. The unsuitability of Amesbury for an architect's home is specially provided for by Dickens making Pecksniff a teacher, and distinctly stating that "of his architectural doings, nothing was clearly known, except that he had never designed or built anything."

There are two or three coach-roads, as are necessitated by the story, one running from London to Salisbury, without touching Amesbury ; the other running right through Amesbury, and over Salisbury Plain, for the west country. Ignorance of this latter coach route has led some Dickens topographers into difficulties, but with it everything becomes clear. The turnpike house exists, at which Tom left his box, and the church at which he played the organ (Chap. II.) is a fine old structure, and though there is no wall through a wood from the house we have selected as Pecksniff's, there is a path through a little plantation which would make quite a short cut

MIDDLE TEMPLE LANE.

"You couldn't meet me at the Temple Gate in Fleet Street in an hour from this time, could you ?"
—*Chuzzlewit.*

to the north-west corner of the churchyard. There is not a " descent of two steps on the inside" of the bedroom behind the Dragon, but one of the rooms in the George has a descent of one step, quite enough to trip an unwary person.

Tom Pinch's journey to Salisbury to meet Martin Chuzzlewit was along a charming undulating road, and the inn where he waited in the High Street, not far from the north gate of the Cathedral close, may still be seen, though it is no longer used as an inn. The Cathedral, with its tall, graceful spire, is a beautiful object, when seen "from the north. From the south. From the east. From the west. From the south-east. From the nor'-west," —as Mr. Pecksniff showed it, in students' elevations in the work-room on the eve of Martin's arrival.

We have located Mr. Pecksniff's house on the road to Wilsford, and as the coach over Salisbury Plain came down the road from

THE MIDDLE TEMPLE, FOUNTAIN COURT.

"Brilliantly the Temple Fountain sparkled in the sun, and laughingly its liquid music played, and merrily the idle drops of water danced and danced as little Ruth and her companion came towards it."—*Chuzzlewit*.

Stonehenge, it would be necessary to walk to "the finger-post at the end of the lane" to take it. Mr. Pecksniff went by "the heavy coach," while Martin must have come to Salisbury by the mail, hence, Tom's journey to fetch him.

The coach-office in the City, and Mrs. Todgers' boarding-house cannot be identified, though Mr. Allbut states (on what authority we know not) that King's Head Court, Fish Street Hill, is the "kind of paved yard" where Mrs. Todgers kept her Commercial Boarding House. Certainly, from the top of any of the houses in this court

one could see "if the day were bright, upon the house-tops, stretch-
ing far away, a long dark path: the shadow of the Monument: and
turning round, the tall original was close beside you, with every hair
erect upon his golden head, as if the doings of the city frightened

him." We shall
search Camberwell
in vain for the house
of "the wealthiest
brass and copper
founder known to
mankind," and
though there are still
"some very narrow
streets somewhere
behind the Post-
Office," none of their
buildings answers the
description of that
occupied by Anthony
Chuzzlewit and Son,
Manchester Ware-
housemen.

KINGSGATE STREET, HOLBORN.

"The best of blessings in a sick room is Mrs. Gamp. Send a boy to
Kingsgate Street and snap her up at any price."—*Chuzzlewit.*

"A famous Inn!" where John Westlock entertained Tom Pinch,
was doubtless the White Hart in St. John Street, the best house in
Salisbury. Martin's tramp and ride, to Hounslow, and London, can
easily be followed, but "the humbler regions of the Adelphi," rich
in memories of Dickens's own humbler days, are swept away. We
may still see couples meet in St. James's Park, as Martin met Mary
Graham, and our view of the open space where they talked shows
the Horse Guards clock which claimed Mark Tapley's attention
(Chap. XIV.). The voyage on the *Screw* is more or less reminiscent
of Dickens's own trip, though it lands the travellers in New York,
instead of Boston.

Kingsgate Street, High Holborn, home of the immortal Sairey
Gamp, has gone, alas! in the year of grace 1902; Mr. Mould's place

"within the ward of Cheap" is insufficiently described for identification; and the Bull, in Holborn, though its front portion still stands, is sadly fallen from its old estate, and is about as featureless as any piece of architecture can be. In Pall Mall we cannot assign any particular rooms as those of Tigg Montague, Esq.; nor can we find the city offices and west end branch of the Anglo-Bengalee Loan Company. Furnival's Inn, where John Westlock lived, has been illustrated and no longer exists. Austin Friars we may still see; and the Temple Gate in Fleet Street, where Tom Pinch was to meet Mr. Fips; and Covent Garden Market, where Tom and Ruth had many a pleasant stroll; and London Bridge, where Mr. Nadgett watched Jonas Chuzzlewit sink the bundle of clothing which, fished up, convicted him of the murder of Tigg Montague; and, best of all, we may still see the Garden Court, Temple, of which Dickens gives one of his most perfectly charming descriptions, and where he lays two of his very prettiest love-scenes, between John Westlock and the gentle Ruth Pinch. Perhaps this chapter cannot close better than with the words at the opening of Chapter LIII. of *Chuzzlewit* :—

"Brilliantly the Temple Fountain sparkled in the sun, and laughingly its liquid music played, and merrily the idle drops of water danced and danced, and peeping out in sport among the trees, plunged lightly down to hide themselves, as little Ruth and her companion came towards it.

"And why they came towards the Fountain at all is a mystery; for they had no business there. It was not in their way. It was quite out of their way. They had no more to do with the Fountain, bless you, than they had with—with Love, or any out of the way thing of that sort."

Canterbury Cathedral. ("David Copperfield.")
By Catharine Weed Barnes Ward.

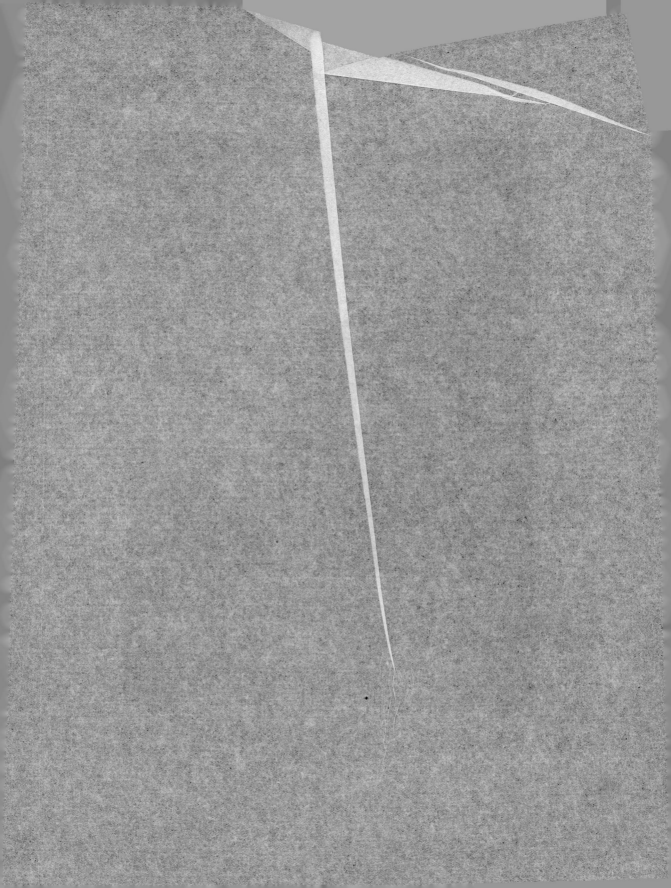

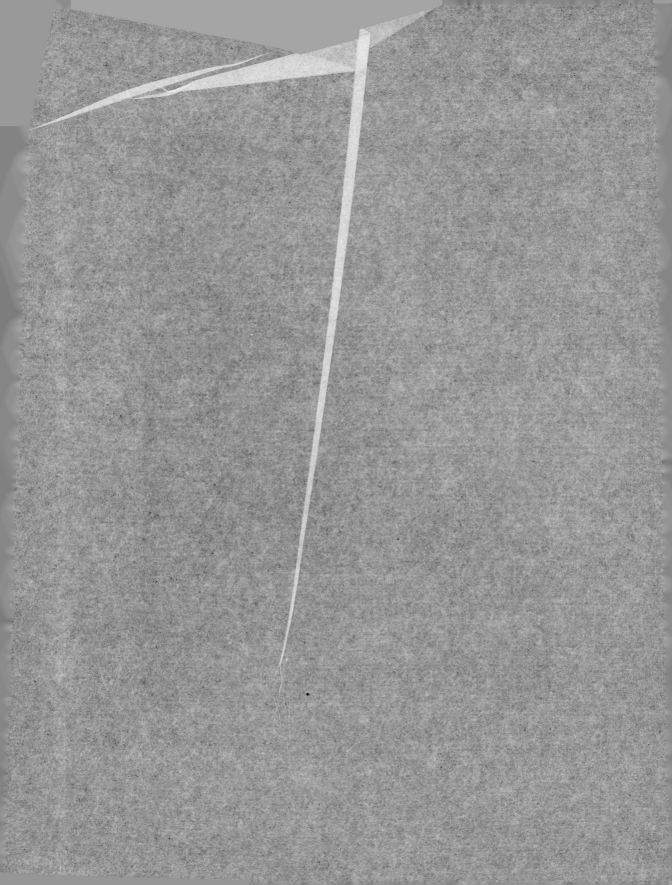

HORNSEY CHURCHYARD.

"To the churchyard at Hornsey, and followed the coffin to a corner I remember well."—*Copperfield*.

CHAPTER VIII

Christmas Books; "Pictures from Italy"; "Dombey and Son"; and "David Copperfield"

LONDON, BRIGHTON, LEAMINGTON, KENILWORTH, BLUNDESTON, YARMOUTH, DOVER, CANTERBURY, ETC., 1843—1850

REST was often sought by Dickens, but even his holidays were rushing, busy times; and our space is too limited to detail the events of the period of "rest" now in view. At the beginning of 1843 Dickens edited and published *Evenings of a Working Man*, for the benefit of John Overs, a poor carpenter who was dying of consumption. He was contributing poems to Lady Blessington's *Keepsake*, political contributions and squibs to the *Chronicle*, superintending the production of a dramatised *Chuzzlewit*, presiding at great meetings in Liverpool,

BELL HARRY
TOWER,
CANTERBURY.

Birmingham, etc., entertaining parties of influential guests and dining out with influential people, and taking a strong, keen interest in the pleasures and education of his children; in addition

GREAT HALL, KNEBWORTH.
Scene of the theatrical performances, 1850, and later; for the Guild of
Literature and Art.

to a great production of literary work.

On January 15th, 1844, his fifth child was born (named Francis Jeffrey). In May, as the Devonshire Terrace House had been let, the family moved into 9, Osnaburgh Terrace, at the corner of Albany Street, for a month or so; and in June, Dickens had a short yachting cruise. At the same time he was raising a testimonial from the Little Portland Street congregation to the Rev. Edward Tagart, as the result of which a large silver salver was presented in July, just after Dickens had started for Italy, sped by a farewell dinner at Greenwich.

The party started for Italy on July 1st, and included Mrs. Dickens, Miss Hogarth, children, courier, and servants. They arrived at Marseilles on the 14th, and were settled in the Villa Bagnerello, Albano, on the 16th. Early in September they were joined by Fred Dickens, who, a few days later, was almost drowned in sight of his friends while bathing. On the first of October they moved to the

Peschiere Palace, Genoa ; and almost the whole of November was spent by Dickens in travelling, to Stradella, Parma, Bologna, Ferrara, Venice, Lodi, and Milan, before taking a quick run over the Alps, and by Fribourg, Strasbourg, and Paris to London, to read the MS. of *The Chimes,* in Forster's rooms, to a small party of friends. In December he spent a few days in Paris on the way to Genoa, which he reached on the 22nd.

On January 20th, 1845, they set out on a tour to the South of Italy— Carrara, Pisa, Rome, Naples, and Florence, returning to Genoa on April 9th. In June they started for home by way of Switzerland, calling at Andermatt, Lucerne, Brussels, and other places, and reaching Devonshire

TEMPLE GARDENS.

"'I felt sure it was you,' said John, when he overtook her in the sanctuary of Garden Court."—*Chuzzlewit.*

Terrace early in July. From August to October 1st they were at Broadstairs, and in September Ben Jonson's *Every Man in his Humour,* was twice produced in Miss Kelly's Theatre, with Dickens as Captain Bobadil. On October 28th, a sixth child was born, and named Alfred Tennyson ; and a couple of days later the second raven, "Grip," died.

Although Dickens was over-worked, ill, and worried, he was busy on plans for a daily paper, and on January 21st, 1846, *The Daily*

News was established under his editorship. He soon wearied, however, of the strain and friction of daily journalism, and on the 9th of February resigned his position to Forster, who held it until the end of the year.

From June to November, 1846, the family lived at Lausanne, whence many trips were taken, including one to Chamounix and the

ALDGATE PUMP.
"Oh! well might Mr. Toots leave the little company . . . to take a little turn to Aldgate Pump and back."—*Dombey*.

glaciers ; and one to the Great St. Bernard, which was afterwards described in *Little Dorrit*. And, curiously enough, the first public reading ever given by Dickens was a reading of a part of *Dombey and Son* at Lausanne. In November they returned to Paris, and took a house in the Rue de Courcelles, where they stayed until the end of February, 1847, save for a trip to London, by Dickens himself, from December 15th to 23rd.

On returning from Paris in 1847, a house was taken in Chester Place, Regent's Park, and there, on April 18th, the seventh child and fifth son was born, and named Sydney Smith Haldimand. The summer and autumn were spent at Brighton and Broadstairs, with breaks for great theatrical performances at Manchester and Liverpool for charitable purposes—the play, *Every Man in his Humour*, stage manager, Charles Dickens, and cast including John Forster, Mark Lemon, Douglas Jerrold, John Leech, George Cruikshank, and two of Dickens's brothers. In December, Dickens presided at great meetings in Leeds and Glasgow.

The year 1848 saw more performances for charity, when Dickens produced *The Merry Wives of Windsor* at the Haymarket before influential audiences, which on one occasion included Queen Victoria and Prince Albert; and took his company to Manchester, Liverpool, Birmingham, Edinburgh, and Glasgow. The summer and autumn were spent at Broadstairs again, and part of the winter at Brighton. On the 5th of July Dickens was summoned to the death-bed of his sister Fanny, to whom he was devotedly attached.

On January 7th, 1849, Dickens went to Yarmouth and district, including visits to Norwich and Stanfield Hall, for "local colour" for *David Copperfield*.

On January 6th the eighth child was born, christened Henry Fielding; and now the eminent King's Counsel and Recorder of Maidstone.

About this time the widow of Seymour published a statement that her husband had originated *Pickwick*, and claimed for him some considerable share of the credit, but the idea was shown to be baseless. Dickens wrote largely in *The Times* against public executions and greatly helped the crusade for making them private. In February, the family, with Miss Hogarth and Mr. and Mrs. Leech, stayed for some time in Brighton, in the spring and autumn they were

THE WOODEN MIDSHIPMAN.
"Affectionately patting him on one leg of his knee-shorts for old acquaintance sake."— *Uncom. Trav.*

at Broadstairs, and for the summer they took a house at Bonchurch, Isle of Wight. During this year Dickens's eldest son entered Eton, and Dickens himself "ate his dinners" in the Middle Temple, which he had entered in 1839. In November Mr. and Mrs. Dickens were of the house party at Rockingham Castle, when the novelist was the heart and soul of a dramatic performance and other entertainments.

In 1850 the spring was spent in Brighton, and the late summer and autumn again at Broadstairs, but in this year Dickens began to complain of the itinerant musicians, and his attachment for the North

L

Kentish watering-place was greatly shaken.   In January there was a visit to Rockingham Castle, with private theatricals.   August 16th saw the birth of a third daughter, and ninth child (Dora Annie); and in November there was a series of theatrical performances at Lord Lytton's home at Kneb-worth, in aid of the Guild of Literature and Art.

ST. DUNSTAN'S, FLEET STREET.
"High up in the steeple, far above the light and murmur of the town . . . dwelt the Chimes."—*The Chimes.*

A series of Christmas books (distinct from the Christmas stories, of the next decade) was published in the years 1843–1848, and like most of Dickens's ventures, proved a great success. Of the first, *A Christmas Carol*, published in December, 1843, 15,000 copies were sold, and £726 were paid to the author as his share of the profits, but he expressed bitter disappointment because he had expected a full £1,000. The books, and the stories which followed them, carried the Christmas spirit of peace and goodwill into homes all over the world, and so great was their effect that the feeling at the time of Dickens's death was well typified by a little girl who asked her parents—"Is Father Christmas dead, too?"

The Christmas books are but slightly localised, though there are many incidental place-references, to St. Paul's Churchyard, the Mansion House, etc.   An old knocker on a door in Craven Street, Strand, is believed to be the one that suggested the fancy of Scrooge's knocker (in *A Christmas Carol*) changing into Marley's face; but we understand that the request of a photographer for permission to photograph the knocker led the lady of the house to have it removed, and stored in her banker's safe deposit. Bob Cratchit, like so many of Dickens's poor people, lived in Camden Town, and passed through Cornhill on the way to his home. How many people would give much to see the home where Tiny Tim cried, "God bless us, every one," but the indications are not sufficient for its identification.

The Chimes, published in December, 1844, did not cause so much excitement as the *Carol* had done, but it sold well; and the terms with the publishers were better, so that the author realised £1,500 from the sale of 25,000 copies. No localities are clearly identified, but we believe it is a fact that the chimes in Dickens's mind were those in the beautiful lantern-tower of St. Dunstan's, which picturesquely dominates the top of Fleet Street.

The Cricket on the Hearth (December, 1845) was printed and published by Bradbury and

MR. DOMBEY'S HOUSE.

"There was a labyrinth of scaffolding raised all round the house . . . nothing but workmen swarming from the kitchen to the garrets."—*Dombey*.

Evans, under the agreement already mentioned; as was *The Battle of Life* (December, 1846), and *The Haunted Man* (December, 1848), and these have very few local references. Mrs. Swidger (in *The Haunted Man*) casually refers to Battersea, and to various bridges, from London to Hammersmith. The place of business of A. Tetterby and Co., Newsmen, was the corner shop in Jerusalem Buildings, and though we can find no Jerusalem Buildings now, there is a Jerusalem Passage, St. John's Square, Clerkenwell, which would be in many ways suitable for the

L 2

Tetterby scene; and was just the sort of place to be hunted out by Dickens.

Pictures from Italy, the result of the Italian wanderings, was first published in *The Daily News* under the title of "Travelling Sketches," and was reprinted in book form in 1846. The scenes therein described fall outside our present province.

MARYLEBONE CHURCH.
" The church beneath which lies the dust of little Paul and his mother."—*Dombey*.

Dombey and Son is fairly well localised, but unfortunately some of the most interesting places (the Stagg's Garden district, to wit) have been removed for the northern railways. Mr. Dombey's house is not perfectly identified, but it is between Portland Place and Bryanston Square, and Allbut points out a house at the corner of Mansfield Street and Queen Anne Street as exactly corresponding to Dickens's somewhat detailed description. This it does, save in one respect,—it is on the north or sunny side, while Dickens describes it as being on the shady side. The offices of Dombey and Son were in the city, within sound of Bow Bells, within ten minutes' walk of Gog and Magog, close to the Royal Exchange and Bank of England, and "just round the corner" from "the rich East India House," but this description is insufficient for exact identification.

Marylebone Church was the scene of Paul Dombey's christening and burial, and of the second marriage of Mr. Dombey, to Edith Granger. Walter Gay and Florence Dombey walked around here to see the monument to little Paul, on the morning of their wedding-day. Princess's Place is not to be found in the directories, nor is Princess's Chapel nor Princess's Arms, so that we can scarcely hope to find the rooms of Miss Tox or Major Bagstock. Mrs. Pipchin's "Castle," in a steep by-street of Brighton, seems equally undiscoverable.

Leamington, with its Royal Hotel and its pump-room, gives us scenes as characteristic, in their way, as the Bath scenes in *Pickwick*,

MARYLEBONE CHURCH.   INTERIOR.

" Miss Tox in the gallery shrinks behind the fat leg of a cherub on a monument. . . . Captain Cuttle, on the contrary, stands up and waves his hook, in token of welcome and encouragement."—*Dombey and Son.*

but the style has settled from boisterous fun to quiet and even satirical humour, and we feel that the visit is made in very different company from that of the simple-minded Pickwick, and the astute, illiterate Sam Weller. The rides to Warwick Castle and to Kenilworth introduce us to beautiful scenes,—some of the fairest in fair old England,—and pave the way for Mr. Dombey's second marriage, for which Mrs. Skewton borrows a house in Brook Street, Grosvenor Square. We have referred to Marylebone Church, but must mention it again, in connection with Chapter XXXI., with its wonderful detailed description of the wedding.

The contrasted homes of James Carker at Norwood, and of John and Harriet Carker somewhere on the Great North Road (probably about Finchley), are not identifiable.

When the wedding of Walter and Florence is being arranged,

KENILWORTH CASTLE.
"Dombey projected this morning a ride to Warwick Castle and to Keni'.worth."—*Dombey and Son.*

they select "a mouldy old church in a yard, hemmed in by a labyrinth of back streets and courts," and somewhere in the city, far from St. Marylebone, where they call to see Paul's tablet. We cannot find the mouldy church, but we find an echo of Dickens's own honeymoon when they decide to "go away that morning, and stay in Kent until we go aboard at Gravesend within a week."

Everyone who has read *Dombey* loves good Captain Cuttle and the Little Midshipman, and it is pleasant to know that every day during business hours, the wooden figure may be seen taking his observations outside the shop of Norie and Wilson, ships' instrument makers, 156, Minories; to which he removed, with his firm, from 157, Leadenhall Street. No. 9, Brig Place, home of Mrs. Mac Stinger, is not to be found by the India Docks, though we may still see a Cautious Clara moored off Ratcliff.

Amongst the casual and minor references are some to Peckham, where Walter went to a weekly boarding school; the Mile-End turn-pike to which a woman asked her way, making one of the two people who had entered Sol Gills's shop in ten days; the City Road, near which little Biler was taught at the Charitable Grinders'; Thames Street, where Walter was check-ing the shipping of some goods and first met Florence Dombey, who had wandered away from home and been lost; Rottingdean, where Miss Pankey's aunt lived; Bishopsgate Street Without,

KENILWORTH. ENTRANCE TO BANQUET-HALL.
"The castle is charming!—associations of the Middle Ages—and all that."—*Dombey*.

with the shop of "one Brogley, sworn broker and appraiser," round the corner from Sol Gills's; Hampstead, to which Walter walked (past Mr. Dombey's house) to see the fields; Ball's Pond, where dwelt Perch, the messenger; Oxford Market, where Mr. Towlinson had "visions of leading an altered and blameless exist-ence as a serious green-grocer"; Fulham, with the pretty villa of Sir Barnet and Lady Skettles; Finchley, to which Mr. Toots went for "some uncommonly fine chickweed for Miss Dombey's bird," and an undefined place in Essex where Susan Nipper's brother was a farmer.

David Copperfield was issued in monthly parts from May, 1849, to November, 1850; and was very largely autobiographical. Many

BLUNDESTONE CHURCH.

" I am so frightened that they are obliged to take me out of bed and show me the quiet churchyard, out of the bedroom window."—*Copperfield.*

traits of Mr. Micawber were drawn from John Dickens, Steerforth had his prototype in George Stroughill, of childhood's days in Chatham, Dora was drawn from a real person, and there is reason to believe that Agnes was a portrait of a lady, still living. David was almost entirely Dickens, and after the story was well under way he noticed the curious coincidence that the initials of the fictitious David were his own, reversed. The Murdstone and Grinby business was drawn from the period of servitude with Warren's blacking, and

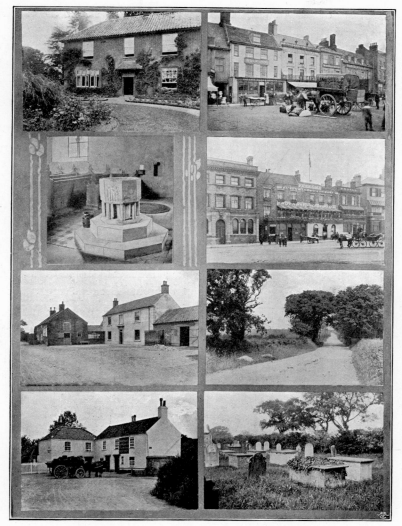

"COPPERFIELD" SCENES IN YARMOUTH DISTRICT.

"THE ROOKERY, BLUNDERSTONE."	MARKET SQUARE, YARMOUTH.
FONT IN BLUNDESTONE CHURCH.	CROWN AND ANCHOR, YARMOUTH.
THE PLOUGH INN, BLUNDESTONE.	ROAD TO YARMOUTH.
THE INN AT HOPTON.	BLUNDESTONE CHURCHYARD.

many, even of the small details were drawn from the author's memory,—not his imagination.

Blunderstone is really Blundestone, some seven miles from Yarmouth, to which there is a good slightly undulating highway, with a good country inn (the Plough) at Blundestone, whence Mr.

THE OBELISK, ST. GEORGE'S FIELDS.
"A long-legged young man, with a very little empty donkey-cart, standing near the Obelisk."—*Copperfield.*

Barkis started in his carrier's cart, and another, halfway, at Hopton, where he stopped on the way. "The Rookery' was undoubtedly the vicarage, for it could be seen from the church, whereas Blundestone Hall, sometimes identified as the original of the Rookery, is too far away, and the view is blocked. In describing the church, Dickens was not so accurate as was his wont, for he spoke of its spire, whereas it has one of the very few round towers to be found in England,—of the pattern so common in Ireland. And he wrote of Peggotty seeing the Rookery from the church, which is impossible, because the windows in the church are very high.

Lowestoft is entirely changed since Mr. Murdstone took David there and met "Mr. Brooks, of Sheffield." Peggotty's boat-hut had probably many originals, for in the allotment gardens that once flourished around Yarmouth, many old boats were used as tool-sheds and shelters. The one known as Peggotty's hut (no one seems quite sure whether it was there before the book was written) was on the spit of land between the river and the sea, near Nelson's monument. There are two or three old hostelries from which coaches started for London, and carriers' carts for villages around Yarmouth, and to this day there are few parts of England in which the carriers' carts are so largely used.

Salem House, "down by Blackheath," was probably imaginary, but the characters were largely drawn from the Wellington House Academy.

Though the Murdstone and Grinby place is said to have been "down in Blackfriars," we know well that it was really near Hungerford Stairs, now swept away, but fortunately the upper part of

CANTERBURY CATHEDRAL.

"Stray rooks and jackdaws come down from the Cathedral towers to walk with a clerkly bearing on the grass-plot."—*Copperfield.*

City Road is still very much as it was when Mr. Micawber gave his address at Windsor Terrace, there. The story of how "I board myself" (Chap. XI.) describes Dickens's own boyish struggles, and the places centre around Hungerford Stairs, not around Blackfriars;

and the other story, of the Micawbers' troubles, is drawn from personal experience.

The tramp to Dover is one of the most pathetic things in Dickens's works; with the long-legged young man near the Obelisk, who stole his money and box; Mr. Dolloby, who bought his waist-

CITY ROAD, LONDON.

"My address," said Mr. Micawber, "is Windsor Terrace, City Road. I—in short . . . I live there."
—*Copperfield.*

coat, in the Kent Road; Salem House, where he slept beside a haystack; the Sunday trudge of twenty-three miles along the Dover Road, past the honeymoon cottage at Chalk, and past Gadshill; sleeping near a cannon on the battery at Chatham; the sale of the little jacket to the "goroo" man; the sunny street of Canterbury; the terrible struggle forward to Dover; the heartless replies of the men from whom he enquired his aunt's address; and his kindly reception by that eccentric woman, whose home is not certainly identifiable.

We are not entirely satisfied with the identification of Mr. Wickfield's, or Dr. Strong's, or the little inn, where Micawber stayed, or the County inn, where Mr. Dick stayed on alternate Wednesdays.

Mr. Allbut identifies everything without the slightest hesitation, but also, as it seems to us, without sufficient grounds.   Other people are equally confident about totally different places, and we doubt whether the Canterbury scenes were exactly placed in Dickens's own mind.   The beautiful Bell Harry Tower, at any rate, admits of no doubt.

The Steerforth house and Dr. Strong's cottage at High-gate, and the little home where David settled with his "child-wife" cannot be identified; Doctors' Commons is gone, save for a small part remaining as the house of the Dean of St. Paul's; but Mrs. Crupp's lodg-ings, where Dickens really did lodge, still stands, the bottom house on the left hand side of Buckingham Street, Adelphi. The Piazza Hotel (the Tavi-stock), Covent Garden, where Steerforth met some friends; Ely Place, Holborn, where Mr. Wickfield's agent lived; the

MRS. CRUPP'S LODGINGS.

"A furnished little set of Chambers in the Adelphi, Trot, ought to suit you to a marvel."—*Copperfield.*

clock of St. Andrew's, Holborn, by which David timed his appoint-ment with Agnes; Covent Garden, where he bought a bouquet for Dora; the Roman bath, just out of the Strand; Hampstead Heath; the steps of St. Martin's-in-the-Fields, where David met Martha and Mr. Peggotty during the search for Emily; Putney Common, where he strolled with Dora; Golden Square, near which Emily was found; the churchyard at Hornsey, where Betsy Trot-wood's husband was buried in a well-remembered corner (there is only one corner, in fact); No. 2, Holborn Court, Gray's Inn, where

Traddles lived while poor, and the Temple, where he worked when success was gained; these, and many other places incidentally mentioned, remain with little change.

ELY PLACE, HOLBORN.

"My dear Trotwood, I am staying at the house of papa's agent, Mr. Waterbrook, in Ely Place."—*Copperfield*.

The house of Mr. Spenlow, in Norwood, the house at Putney, where David visited with Dora, and the little chandler's shop in Hungerford Market, over which Mr. Peggotty found rooms, are past identification. Castle Street, Holborn, though it still remains under the name of Furnival Street, has had so many of its houses rebuilt that we cannot identify the one behind the parapet of which Traddles found a lodging; and the waterside at Millbank, where Martha contemplated suicide, has changed out of all recognition since Millbank Prison gave place to the Tate Gallery, and other great Westminster improvements have taken place.

TOMB IN ROCKINGHAM CHURCH.

"On Sunday the chill little church is almost warmed by so much gallant company, and the general flavour of the Dedlock dust is quenched in delicate perfumes."—*Bleak House.*

CHAPTER IX

"Household Words," "A Child's History of England," "Bleak House," "Hard Times," and "Little Dorrit"

LONDON, ST. ALBANS, ROCKINGHAM, MANCHESTER, THE MARSHALSEA PRISON, ETC., 1850–1859.

A S early as 1845 Dickens had the idea of starting a periodical, owned, edited, and entirely controlled by himself, through which he might not only publish his novels, but also the stories, short articles, and other writings of people whose philanthropic and humanitarian ideas were like his own. Names suggested for it were,— *The Cricket, The Robin, Mankind, Charles Dickens,* and many others, but at last, *Household Words* was decided upon. Its proprietary

BEAUFORT ARMS, BATH.

was a partnership between Dickens, John Forster, W. H. Wills (sub-editor, and a most devoted friend of Dickens), and Bradbury and Evans, the printers.   The first number was published on March 30th, 1850.   On May 16th, 1859, owing to a regrettable piece

of personal feeling on Dickens's part, the property was sold under an order in Chancery, so that the partnership might be wound up.   It was bought on behalf of Charles Dickens for £3,500, and he issued its final number on May 28th, 1859 ; and merged its interests in *All the Year Round*, which he had established a few months before.

In February, 1851, Dickens visited Paris with John Leech, and in March he took his wife, who was in ill-health, to Malvern.   He had two serious bereavements just at this time, for his father died on March 31st, and on April 14th his baby, Dora Annie, died suddenly in her nurse's arms.

OFFICE OF "HOUSEHOLD WORDS," 16, WELLINGTON STREET, STRAND.

From the beginning of May to November, Dickens was at Broadstairs, making his longest and his last visit to the place.   The theatrical performances for the Guild of Literature and Art were revived in Devonshire House, Piccadilly, in the Hanover Square Rooms, and in the provinces.   On April 30th Queen Victoria was present at the performance.

In October, 1851, the family moved to Tavistock House (now pulled down), where the great room on the first floor made a theatre in which private plays were produced with greater enthusiasm than ever before. At about this time the writing of *A Child's History of England* (written for his own children) was completed.

In 1852 a house at Dover was hired for three months in the summer, and later, Dickens, with his wife and Miss Hogarth, made a short visit to Boulogne. Many "Guild" performances were given in great provincial towns. *Bleak House* began publication in March; and was completed in September of the following year. On the 13th of March, a seventh son, and tenth child (Edward Bulwer Lytton) was born; and in September, when Dickens's theatrical company was playing in Manchester, the opportunity was seized to

OLD CHANCERY COURT.

"This is the Court of Chancery, which has its decaying houses and its blighted lands in every shire."—*Bleak House.*

induce Dickens, Lord Lytton, and Thackeray to take part in the inauguration of the Free Library movement in that city.

On Twelfth Night, 1853, Dickens was the subject of a banquet and presentation in Birmingham; in May or June he went to Brighton, and in June to Boulogne, for the summer and early autumn, whence, on the 10th of October, he started for Switzerland and Italy

M

with Wilkie Collins and Augustus Egg.   In the middle of December the English public readings began, with *A Christmas Carol* on the 27th and 30th, and *The Cricket on the Hearth* on the 29th, in Birmingham.

In January, 1854, the readings were continued, at Birmingham, Bradford, etc., but this did not make Dickens too busy for his children's theatricals on Twelfth Night.   On April 1st *Hard Times* was begun in *Household Words*.   It was a story with a purpose, based on "philanthropical radicalism," and to get suitable local colour Dickens visited Preston, Lancs., during a strike.   In June the summer visit to Boulogne began, and in July *Hard Times* was finished.

Early in 1855 Dickens began a note-book in which to enter memoranda for *Little Dorrit* and other stories, thus showing a first effort to ensure against the results of brain fag which had rendered the writing of *Bleak House* a most difficult

CHICHESTER RENTS.
In which stood the Ship Tavern; supposed to be the original of the "Sol's Arms" of *Bleak House*.

task.   In February he had a fortnight in Paris with Wilkie Collins; but just before doing so, on the 10th, he went with W. H. Wills, "strongly booted," to look over Gadshill Place, which was for sale.   In May the writing of *Little Dorrit* began, and it was not finished until May, 1857. The summer of 1855 was spent at Albion Villas, Folkestone, where John Leech was one of many welcome guests; and in October Dickens was in Paris for some days. In November he removed the family to Paris, where they

TOOK S ("COOK'S") COURT.

" In Cook's Court, Cursitor Street, Mr. Snagsby, Law-
Stationer, pursues his lawful calling."—*Bleak House.*

stayed until the middle of May, 1856; one of the objects being to assist in the production of a French translation of Dickens's works. On March 14th (a Friday, as it happened) the purchase of Gadshill was completed, the first intention being to use it as a summer residence only. From June to September (1856) were again spent in Boulogne, with frequent brief trips to London, Dover, and Gadshill, where Dickens made his

THAVIES INN.

" Don't be frightened. One of the young Jellyby's
been and got his head through the area railings."
—*Bleak House.*

occasional head-quarters at the Falstaff Inn, during alterations and improvements at Gadshill Place, notably the driving of a deep well.

The private theatricals at Tavistock House increased in interest and importance, until the illustrated papers of the period began to treat a first night in Dickens's first-floor room to a couple of half-page illustrations as well as a long critical description. Wilkie Collins's play of *The Frozen Deep* was produced

M 2

here on January 6th, 1857, and during the play Dickens had the first suggestion for *A Tale of Two Cities*, with which a later chapter will deal.

In February, 1857, possession was taken of the renovated Gadshill Place, and here *Little Dorrit* was finished. In July, the first child left the home nest, when Walter Landor, who had obtained his cadet-ship and been edu-cated for the Indian service through the kindness of Miss Coutts (later the Baroness Burdett-Coutts), sailed for India. In Septem-ber, Dickens and Wilkie Collins took a holiday in Cumber-land, returning by Lancaster and Don-caster.

On April 29th, 1858, the first public reading for Dickens's own benefit took place in St. Martin's Hall, and was fol-lowed by fifteen nights between that date and the 22nd of July. Before this, ever since the first public reading, Dickens had been steadily more and more in demand for readings, speeches, and other efforts on behalf of charitable and social objects, and this, added

58, LINCOLN'S INN FIELDS.
"Here, in a large house, formerly a house of state, lives Mr. Tulkinghorn."
—*Bleak House.*

ROCKINGHAM CASTLE ("CHESNEY WOLD"). GARDEN FRONT.

"Sir Leicester and Lady Dedlock are in their happy home, and there is hospitality at the place in Lincolnshire."—*Bleak House*.

THE LONG DRAWING-ROOM, CHESNEY WOLD (ROCKINGHAM).

"Of all the shadows in Chesney Wold, the shadow in the long drawing-room upon my lady's picture is the first to come, the last to be disturbed."—*Bleak House*.

to his enormous amount of literary work, correspondence, and family and personal affairs, kept him in a state of constant nervous tension, dangerous to even the strongest constitution. The first provincial reading tour, of eighty-seven readings, began at Clifton on August 2nd, 1858, and closed on November 13th, 1858. A few extra readings, in London, about Christmas time, were added.

"THE STREET," ROCKINGHAM CASTLE.

"The long stables in a barren courtyard, where there is a great bell in a turret and a clock with a large face."—*Bleak House.*

A Child's History of England, of course, calls for no description of its scenes, but *Bleak House* introduces us to a large series of places, most of them identifiable, and many of them still existing, connected with most interesting incidents. It is unfortunate that Bleak House itself cannot be pointed out, although the description of its position is given with apparent exactness. We conclude that Dickens had no actual house in his mind; and it is ridiculous to assert, as has been done, that the description of the house was in any way based upon Fort House, Broadstairs, or upon Cobley's Farm (Fallow Farm), Finchley, where Dickens is said to have stayed during the writing of a portion of the book. Bleak House was "near St. Albans . . . out of the town, round a corner . . . on the top of a hill before us." It was "up an avenue of trees" which the carriage "turned into," and was an "old-fashioned house, with three peaks in the roof in front, and a circular sweep leading to the porch," and Miss Summerson's window looked upon "a cheerful landscape, prominent in which the old Abbey Church, with its massive tower, threw a softer train of shadow on the view than seemed compatible with its rugged character."

The old Court of Chancery still remains in Lincoln's Inn ; and curiously enough, after being disused for Chancery purposes for some twenty-five years,

THE KEEPER'S LODGE.
" The dark beauty of this lodge, standing in a twilight of trees, and how the ivy clustered over it."—*Bleak House.*

after being said to be doomed to removal, even after being described as actually removed, it is again in use for Chancery business.

MR. GEORGE'S LODGE.
"In . . . that lodge, within sight of the house, . . . the stalwart man, the trooper formerly, is housed."—*Bleak House.*

Cook's Court, Cursitor Street—really called Took's Court—retains the old houses of one side, one of which (the nearest to Cursitor Street) we selected as being most likely to be Mr. Snagsby's. As we were preparing to photograph this, a small boy hung uneasily around, and finally asked if he might be "took" at the same time, and his address, volunteered in reply to our offer to send him a print, was a house in Chichester Rents ! A curious coincidence, for the Old Ship Tavern, once standing at the corner of Chichester Rents, was the Sol's Arms of Dickens, the scene of the inquest on Nemo.

Lincoln's Inn has had some new buildings since the "fifties," but ample space remains in Old Square for the offices of Kenge and Carboy, and in the "Fields" beyond still stands No. 58, the house of John Forster, and also of Mr. Tulkinghorn.   Much of Thavies

NO. 26, NEWMAN STREET.

"Determined to be taught to dance, so I went to Mr. Turveydrop's Academy in Newman Street."—*Bleak House.*

Inn remains unchanged, and we have photographed No. 8, not because it is definitely described as the Jellyby's house, but because it is the first that answers the description of Miss Summerson's introduction, with the railings and the area below; and because it is opposite the place where the beadle of the Inn sometime had his cosy box. Krook's shop, at the end of Bishop's Court, has been replaced by a new building quite recently.

Old Street, or Old Street Road, the residence of Mrs. Guppy, has altered much, but Penton Place, Pentonville Road, where Mr. Guppy lived in lodgings, retains its old style; and fortunately for us, Mr. Snagsby's favourite haunt, Staple Inn, still invites the traveller to wander through its portal from Holborn and "to observe how countrified the sparrows and the leaves are." Coavinses' Castle, the sheriff's officer's house, where poor "gentlemen under a cloud" were lodged, has gone from Chancery Lane, with the system that rendered it possible and necessary.

Mr. Turveydrop's Academy, in Newman Street, Oxford Street, can easily be identified as No. 26, because that is the only house "at the corner of an archway" and with a room built out in the rear that would answer for the dancing academy.   Bell Yard, where

Neckett, the father of "Charley," and the "man from Shropshire" lived, and to which Miss Flite moved after the death of Krook, has been quite altered by the building of the new Law Courts, and the

ROCKINGHAM CASTLE ("CHESNEY WOLD"). THE GREAT HALL.
Wherein Dickens produced plays and led the revels on more than one occasion.

two or three old houses remaining are much too good for the residence of such poor people.

Tom-all-Alone's is gone, and its site is now covered by a continuation of York Street, Covent Garden.

The "rather ill-favoured and ill-savoured neighbourhood," where "one of its rising grounds bears the name of Mount Pleasant," is close to the Field Lane of Fagin's haunting, and has been immensely improved by the laying out of Rosebery Avenue and the rebuilding of much of the adjoining property. It was a fit abode for the noxious Smallweed family, and some of the better class of the old houses still remain in Mount Pleasant and neighbouring streets. Mr. George's shooting gallery is beyond identification, nor can we be sure of that "street of little shops" near the Elephant and Castle, in front of one of which Mrs. Bagnet was found "as usual, washing greens." Hatton Garden has many a house to which Jellyby's might have moved after the father of the family "became a shorn lamb"; and in passing we may remark that Caddy and her husband, like

ALBION VILLAS, FOLKESTONE.
Summer residence of the Dickens family in 1855 and later.

Dickens and his wife, chose the neighbourhood of Gravesend for their wedding-trip.

Clifford's Inn, where Melchisedechs did business for Mr. Smallweed, is doomed to fall shortly, Mr. Vholes's place, Symond's Inn, went long ago, and Mr. Skimpole's home in the Polygon has also vanished.

Deal, where Esther went to meet Richard Carstone, preserves much of its old quaintness, and sailing ships still lie in the Downs as Richard's did, although the general use of steam has lessened their numbers.

And what of Chesney Wold? There, Dickens has entirely put us off the scent by his constant references to "the place in Lincolnshire," but we know, on the very best authority, that the house actually in his mind was Rockingham Castle; the village of Chesney Wold was the village of Rockingham, and the Dedlock Arms was the Sondes' Arms. The long drawing-room, the library, the terrace, with the Ghost's Walk, Mr. Tulkinghorn's tower with its flagstaff, the keeper's lodge where Mr. George was installed after the

THE LAST OF TOM ALL ALONE'S DISTRICT.

In the Clare Market neighbourhood, and close to where poor Joe's churchyard stood. Pulled down in 1903.

catastrophe of the story,—all these can easily be found. There are one or two detail discrepancies. The vicarage, which should be Mr. Boythorn's house, is much too near the castle to allow for the right-of-way disputes, and the church almost adjoins the castle, making it practically impossible for "my lady" to drive to the service. But the castle and park are capable of fully realising Dickens's descriptions of the drip, drip of the rain on the Ghost's Walk, and of the glorious expanse and sunshine of other scenes.

A host of minor references are to be found in *Bleak House*; all taking us to real places, though some are vague. There are the "cheerful lodgings near Oxford Street, over an upholsterer's shop" (Chap. XIII.); the Horse Guards, where Richard Carstone applied for his Ensign's commission ; Mr. Bucket's aunt's house "next door but two to the old original Bun House," in Chelsea ; the scenes of that wonderfully described night ride by "the archway toll, at Highgate," and through St. Albans ; Westminster Hall, where the Jarndyce and Jarndyce case broke down because the whole estate had been absorbed in costs ; and the "thriving place, pleasantly situated, streams and streets, town and country, mill and moor," in Yorkshire, where Mr. Woodcourt found an opening for his medical skill.

THE MARSHALSEA PRISON.

"A garret, and a Marshalsea garret (*) without compromise, was Little Dorrit's room."—*Little Dorrit*.

There are other minor references, but we shall only mention one, as showing the accuracy of Dickens in his most casual descriptions.

It is where he speaks of Mr. George's walk to the Bagnets' place, "by the cloisterly Temple, and by Whitefriars (there, not without a glance at Hanging-Sword Alley, which would seem to be something in his way), and by Blackfriars Road, Mr. George sedately marches," etc.   This passing notice of Hanging-Sword Alley is one of those proofs of absolute familiarity that can never be worked up from maps or imagination.

Hard Times cannot be localised at all, save that the general atmosphere of Coketown was intended to represent Manchester.

Little Dorrit opens in Marseilles, and has many references to those Italian and Swiss scenes which Dickens studied because he feared his readers might tire of English backgrounds, but which he did not use to any great extent.   The first English introduction is to the Foundling Hospital (close to the early home in Doughty

Street), from which Mr. Meagles had adopted Tattycoram. Arthur Clennam, arriving from Marseilles, by way of Dover, travelled to London in the "Blue-eyed Maid," as the boy Dickens had done, and though we are not told that he was packed in damp straw, we are told that the evening was "gloomy, close, and stale." The house of Mrs. Clennam, down by the riverside, which was to overwhelm Rigaud in its fall, is, of course, not to be found.

The Marshalsea Prison still remains, in part, between St. George's Church, the Borough High Street, Angel Court, and Marshalsea Place, just as it did when Dickens went to see it, about the time of concluding his story. It is partly a factory and partly cottages, some of them doomed to disappear within a few months or perhaps weeks of the time of writing. A part of the churchyard of St. George's is being altered by the County Council to form a "Little

ST. GEORGE'S CHURCH, BOROUGH.
"The church of St. George, in the borough of Southwark."
—*Little Dorrit.*

Dorrit's Playground" for the children of the district, and other much-needed changes are in progress. The church, wherein Little Dorrit was married, and the vestry where she was allowed to sleep when she returned to the Marshalsea too late for admission, may still be seen by visitors, and it is a curious fact that people often ask to be shown the entries of her christening and marriage in the parish register, forgetting that she was a creature of imagination.

Many of the scenes in the Marshalsea are, undoubtedly, drawn from Dickens's own youthful experiences, and the meetings by the

THE VESTRY, ST. GEORGE'S CHURCH.

" Come into the vestry. One of our curiosities mustn't be cold when we have it in our power to warm her up comfortable."—*Little Dorrit.*

Iron Bridge (Southwark Bridge) are recollections of his wanderings there with "the Orfling."

Grosvenor Square still provides many a house possible for the residence of Mr. Tite Barnacle; but Bleeding Heart Yard, which we would much rather have preserved, for the dwelling of the Plornishes, has been rebuilt for warehouse purposes. Mr. Casby's short street off Gray's Inn Road can only be conjecturally marked, and this is to be regretted, for Flora Finching (born Casby) was a portrait drawn by the disillusioned Dickens of the same original, known in his Doctors' Commons days, who sat for Dora, the child-wife in *Copperfield.* Mr. Meagles's house at Twickenham cannot be pointed out with certainty, though more than one place can be found to fairly answer the description. In Harley Street, Cavendish Square, the house of Mr. Merdle was to be found, and may be still, for it is not identified, though the street is very crisply sketched in a few sentences.

Mrs. Gowan's abode, in the private apartments of Hampton Court Palace, is a charming spot. The Strand, where Clennam saw Tatty-coram and Blandois; the Adelphi, and the Terrace, to which he followed them, and where he met Miss Wade, are not much altered, —the Adelphi, not at all.

The incidental place-references are very many; a few worth noting are :— Lad Lane and Wood Street, Cheap-

ST. GEORGE'S CHURCH, INTERIOR.
"They all gave place when the singing was done, and Little Dorrit and her husband walked out of the church."—*Little Dorrit*.

side, where "they come a-racing out at twelve or fourteen mile an hour, them Mails do," as Cavaletto found to his cost ; St. Bartholomew's Hospital, to which he was taken ; Covent Garden, where Clennam took a lodging ; Pentonville, the home of Pancks and Rugg ; the "grave old-fashioned City street, lying not far from the Bank of England, by London Wall," where Doyce and Clennam shared a portion of a roomy house ; the dull by-street, in the Grosvenor Square region, near Park Lane, where Miss Wade lodged ; Monument Yard (presumably intended for Monument Square), with the offices of Messrs. Peddle and Pool, solicitors to Edward Dorrit, Esquire ; Brook Street, Grosvenor Square, where Mr. Dorrit was established by his courier ; the school at Blackheath (? reminiscent of Copperfield's), where Mr. F. had been educated ; the places on Mr. Dorrit's journey, where he was "waylaid at Dartford, pillaged at Gravesend, rifled at Rochester, fleeced at Sittingbourne, and sacked at Canterbury," and we may even still see, what we must not miss,—an ancient pie-shop, in the Borough, "across the road" from the Marshalsea, where Flora Finching apologetically invited Little Dorrit and Mr. F.'s aunt with the words :—

"Painfully aware, Miss Dorrit, I am sure that to propose an adjournment to any place to one so far removed by fortune and so courted and caressed by the best society must ever appear intruding even if not a pie-shop far below your present sphere and a back-parlour though a civil man but if for the sake of Arthur—cannot overcome it more improper now than ever late Doyce and Clennam —one last remark I might wish to make one last explanation I might wish to offer perhaps your good nature might excuse under pretence of three kidney ones the humble place of conversation."

Mr. F.'s aunt herself remarked, at various times, that,—"When we lived at Henley, Barnes's gander was stole by tinkers," that "The Monument near London Bridge was put up after the Great Fire of London ; and the Great Fire of London was not the fire in which your uncle George's workshops was burned down," and again that immortal, irrelevant statement, "there's milestones on the Dover Road."

HAMPTON COURT.   THE PRIVATE APARTMENTS.
"My mother lives in the most primitive manner down in that dreary red-brick dungeon at Hampton Court."
—*Little Dorrit.*

OLD NEWGATE PRISON.

"We shall never forget the feelings of awe and respect with which we used to gaze upon the exterior of Newgate."—*Sketches.*

CHAPTER X

"All the Year Round," "A Tale of Two Cities," "Reprinted Pieces," "The Uncommercial Traveller"

LONDON, PARIS, MISCELLANEOUS.
1859–1860

AMILY troubles were at the bottom of the quarrel between Dickens and his publishers, Bradbury and Evans, and loth as we feel to touch the subject, it is necessary to refer to the darkest episode in our novelist's life, when, as the result of incompatibility growing for some time, he separated from his wife. Writing to Forster, just before the separation, of the circumstances at home, he said,—"Nothing can put *them* right, until we are all dead and buried and risen. It is not, with me, a matter of will, or trial, or

N

THE CRISPIN AND CRISPIANUS.

sufferance, or good humour, or making the best of it, or making the worst of it, any longer. It is all despairingly over. Have no lingering hope of, or for, me in this association. A dismal failure has to be borne, and there an end." The separation took place in May, 1858, the eldest son going with his mother, and the other children

26, WELLINGTON STREET, STRAND.
The office of *All the Year Round.*

remaining with the father, and Miss Hogarth, their aunt, with them. The world need not have known anything of this, but Dickens, stung by malicious gossip, inserted a statement in *Household Words*, and the failure of his printer-partners to insert the same in *Punch*, which they owned, caused the estrangement between them.

These facts belong to the present chapter rather than to the last, because although they took place in 1858 they were the causes of the establishment of *All the Year Round*, the first number of which was published on April 30th, 1859. The new weekly was used as the vehicle

for publishing *A Tale of Two Cities* and *Great Expectations*, which were also published simultaneously, in monthly parts, by Chapman and Hall, to whom the novelist returned after his disagreement with Bradbury and Evans. *All the Year Round* also contained a series of sketches similar to the early ones by "Boz," under the name of *The Uncommercial Traveller.*

Before dealing with the scenes of these writings we must briefly sketch the events of 1859–60. The year '59 opened, as the previous year had closed, with three readings in London, in January, and many other readings followed during the year. In June, Dickens moved to Gadshill for the summer, and in September he was at

NEWGATE.   A DOORWAY IN THE OLD BAILEY.

"'You know the Old Bailey well, no doubt.' . . 'Ye—es, sir,' returned Jerry . . . 'I do know the Bailey.   'Very well.   Find the door where the witnesses go in, and show the door-keeper this note for Mr. Lorry.'"—*Tale of Two Cities.*

Broadstairs for a week. In October there was a series of fourteen provincial readings, and in November *A Tale of Two Cities* was finished. On the last day of the year Dickens was in Wales, making notes of the wreck of the "Royal Charter" for one of his most eloquent and sympathetic descriptions, used as the first paper of *The Uncommercial Traveller.*

On January 28th, 1860, *The Uncommercial Traveller* commenced in *All the Year Round.* On July 27th, Dickens was called to Manchester on the death of his brother Alfred, whose young widow he brought back to London, after making all arrangements for the burial of Alfred on August 1st at Highgate. *Great Expectations* was begun in September. On the third of that month Dickens burned his letters and papers of twenty years' accumulation, prompted thereto by what he considered the misuse of the documents of certain people deceased; and on the next day Tavistock House was handed over to his successor; so that from this time Gadshill became a permanent instead of only a summer residence. In November, Dickens and Wilkie Collins journeyed into Cornwall to make notes for *A Message from the Sea.*

A Tale of Two Cities is by far the most dramatic, and from a purely artistic point of view the best and the strongest of all Dickens's works. In style, in construction, in intention, and in effect, it is altogether different from the books written before and from those that were to be written afterwards. In one respect, however, it is like many of Dickens's other books,—it took a great hold upon him

HANGING-SWORD ALLEY.
'Mr. Cruncher's private lodging in Hanging-Sword Alley, Whitefriars."—*Tale of Two Cities.*

at the time of writing. Just as Little Nell, Paul Dombey, and other characters carried him away, and a desperate struggle with himself was needed to accomplish his artistic purpose, so the story of the sacrifice of Sydney Carton "has had complete possession of me; I have so far verified what is done and suffered in these pages, as that I have certainly done and suffered it myself."

The story opens in a coach on the Dover Road, with glimpses of Shooter's Hill and of Blackheath, and the overtaking of the coach by Jerry Cruncher, a special messenger from the bank of Tellson and Company (recently rebuilt), adjoining Temple Bar, on the south side

TEMPLE BAR : NOW AT THEOBALD'S PARK.

" Tellson's Bank, by Temple Bar, was an old-fashioned place, even in the year one thousand seven hundred and eighty."—*Tale of Two Cities.*

of Fleet Street. Temple Bar, removed stone by stone and re-erected at great expense, now stands at the entrance of Lady Meux's park, at Theobalds, near Waltham Cross, and, since no Government Office or City Corporation was found to preserve the old Bar in one of our London parks, we cannot be too grateful to the wealthy brewer who saved such a relic. The scenes at Dover, the Royal George Hotel, are not of the greatest interest, and those in France are beyond our present scope; but when the first chapter of Book the Second brings us back to Hanging-Sword Alley, the home of Jerry Cruncher, we are in a purely Dickensian scene, with a richly Dickensian character. The alley has been altered by the pulling down of the oldest houses, and the building of printing works in their stead, but still has some of its old individuality. When we went to photograph it, we found one portion blocked by a

KING'S BENCH WALK.   PAPER BUILDINGS ON LEFT.

". . . and having revived himself by twice pacing the pavements of King's Bench Walk and Paper Buildings,
turned into the Stryver chambers."—*Tale of Two Cities*.

OLD ST. PANCRAS CHURCH.

" . . the gravestones . . . looking on like ghosts in white while the church tower itself looked on like the
ghost of a monstrous giant."—*Tale of Two Cities*.

gentleman clad only in trousers and shirt, with a great red-and-yellow earthenware bowl on the pavement before him, a great lump of yellow soap in hand, and brown towel, hair-brush, comb,

and upper garments hung on the railings of the alley, who was busy with his morning ablutions in the public thoroughfare. We wondered whether he found his wife a "aggerawator" who "flopped agin him." Fleet Street is often mentioned, but little of its old aspect remains. Even since 1860 it is almost entirely altered, though we still have the old Cheshire Cheese, probably "the nearest tavern to dine well at," to which Carton led Darnay when,

CARLISLE HOUSE, CARLISLE STREET, SOHO.

"The quiet lodgings of Dr. Manette were in a quiet street corner not far from Soho Square; a quainter corner was not to be found in London."
—Tale of Two Cities.

"drawing his arm through his own, he took him down Ludgate Hill to Fleet Street, and so, up a covered way, into a tavern."

Newgate and the Old Bailey are entirely changed; alas! that Newgate should have been destroyed. Tyburn, too, has left no suggestive traces at what is now the Marble Arch. The Court of King's Bench is housed in the new Law Courts in the Strand, but the Temple, with its King's Bench Walk and Paper Buildings, has suffered little from the hand of time.

The house of Doctor Manette is difficult to discover. Was it purely a fancy picture, or a partly fancy picture woven around a real house, or really an actual picture of a house that is destroyed or altered ? Mr. Allbut asserts that Carlisle House, at the end of Carlisle Street, Soho Square, is the house in question, and that there was a garden behind, which has now been covered with a glass roof and converted into a warehouse. Certainly Carlisle House seems to

ST. SEPULCHRE'S CHURCH.

"The concourse waited with an impatience which increased with every chime of St. Sepulchre's clock."—*Barnaby Rudge*.

answer the purpose better than anything else now to be found in the neighbourhood.

Old St. Pancras Church, in St. Pancras Road, and not to be confounded with St. Pancras Church in Upper Woburn Place, saw the burial of paving-stones to represent Roger Cly, the spy, and the disappointment of the body-snatcher Jerry Cruncher, who was afterwards, in Paris, able to press Barsad into Carton's service by showing that he was the same Roger Cly.

The minor references to places are not very numerous. Shrewsbury School was where Sydney Carton and his exploiting "friend" Stryver first met ; somewhere in Clerkenwell was Mr. Lorry's abode ; Darnay found employment in Cambridge as a teacher of languages ; Warwickshire and Wales were selected as the scenes of the honeymoon trip of Darnay and Lucie ; and their marriage took place "in a neighbouring church" to Soho Square (? St. Giles-in-the-Fields).

Reprinted Pieces is a series of sketches published in *Household Words* at various times, and issued in volume form in 1858. They contain many matters properly falling within the scope of this book, but space forbids our doing more than refer to a few of them. *A Child's Dream of a Star*, one of the most touching of Dickens's minor works, recalls his sister Fanny and the little room over the

THE CRISPIN AND CRISPIANUS, STROOD.

"So should we lie that night at the ancient sign of the Crispin and Crispianus, and rise early next morning to be betimes on tramp again."—*Uncom. Trav.*

doorway of the house on The Brook, at Chatham, overlooking a disused burying-ground. *The Schoolboy's Story* is largely based upon experiences at Wellington House Academy, and partly upon Mr. Giles's school ; *Out of Town* describes Folkestone (Pavilion-stone), just as *Our English Watering-place* deals with Broadstairs. *The Detective Police* speaks feelingly of the office of *Household Words*, —" It is a sultry evening at dusk. The stones of Wellington Street are hot and gritty, and the watermen and hackney-coachmen at the theatre opposite are much flushed and aggravated !" *Down With the Tide* takes us in a police barge to some of the scenes of Rogue Riderhood's working, and *Our School* gives us scenes that are almost entirely of Wellington House origin.

The Uncommercial Traveller is a series of short essays and stories, originally published in *All the Year Round*, and reprinted in book form at various dates, as they became sufficiently numerous. In introducing himself the author says that,—" figuratively speaking, I travel for the house of Human Interest Brothers, and have rather a large connection in the fancy goods way. Literally speaking, I am always wandering here and there from my rooms in Covent Garden, London—now about the City streets, now about the country by-roads —seeing many little things, and some great things, which, because they interest me, I think may interest others."

The first sketch refers to the wreck of the " Royal Charter," and the noble work done by the Rev. Stephen Roose Hughes and the poor people of Llanallgo in tending the bodies, and comforting the kinsfolk of the hundreds of drowned mariners and passengers. The next sketch deals with Wapping Workhouse, with interesting side-references to Aldgate Pump, Wapping Old Stairs, and many similar localities. The Hoxton Britannia Theatre has a brilliant description of its Saturday night performance, and its crowded Sunday service. *Travelling Abroad* introduces us to " a very queer small boy " (Dickens himself) whose words about Gadshill Place are quoted in Chapter I. ; while *City of London Churches* leads us to many a quaint old-world sanctuary,—a pilgrimage that is well worth taking. *Shy Neighbourhoods* describes the creatures,—donkeys, dogs, and fowls,—

inhabiting certain of the lower quarters of London, showing how Dickens's observation of the influence of locality extended beyond the mere human beings.

Tramps (Chapter XI.) makes use of the intimate knowledge of the Dover Road gained by living at Gadshill, and refers to the

CRISPIN AND CRISPIANUS, STROOD.

Showing Dickens's favourite corner seat, from which he could see those who passed by the window.

tramping clock-maker as lodging for the night at the Crispin and Crispianus. An inn of this name in Strood was frequently a place of call on Dickens's own long tramps, for a rest before taking the last couple of uphill miles to his home, and the landlady has told how a certain corner of the settle near the inner door was his favourite seat, because from there he could see the passers by the window ; and how more than once when a poor weary woman with a couple of children has limped past, he has called them in, paid for their refreshment, and sent them away rejoicing with a shilling or two.

Dullborough Town (XII.) gives reminiscences of childhood in Chatham and Rochester, as do *Nurses' Stories* (XV.), *Birthday Celebrations* (XIX.) and *Chatham Dockyard* (XXIV.) ; while a host of interesting glimpses of London are given in *Night Walks* (XIII.), *Arcadian London* (XVI.), *The City of the Absent* (XXI.), and *On an Amateur Beat* (XXXIV.).

Titbulls' Almshouses (XXVII.) must surely be largely, if not altogether, reminiscent of those almshouses on the east side of Bayham Street, nearly opposite to Dickens's sometime home, " commonplace smoky-fronted London almshouses, with a little paved courtyard in front enclosed by iron railings, which have got snowed up, as it were, by bricks and mortar ; which were once in a suburb, but are now in the densely populated town,"—a description as correct to-day as it was when written, though equally applicable to many other almshouses.

The Boiled Beef of New England (XXIII.) reports upon an effort, somewhat on the lines of the recent Alexandra Trust, to provide plain, wholesome meals for poor people, in an establishment founded on a self-supporting basis. The managers " had hired a newly-built warehouse," and the building still stands, unaltered, though turned to other uses, at the corner of Commercial Street and Flower Street. It is not generally known to Dickensians, and it is not a beautiful or a striking building, but it is perhaps worthy the notice of Dickens-lovers as a reminder of one of the many generous and philanthropic schemes that were helped and encouraged by the great novelist, whose heart was ever warm toward the weak and poor and suffering.

GRAVES AT COOLING, KENT.

"As I never saw my father or my mother, my first fancies regarding what they were like, were unreasonably derived from their tombstone."—*Great Expectations*.

CHAPTER XI

"Great Expectations" and "Our Mutual Friend"

COOLING, ROCHESTER, LONDON,
HENLEY-ON-THAMES, ETC.
1860—1865

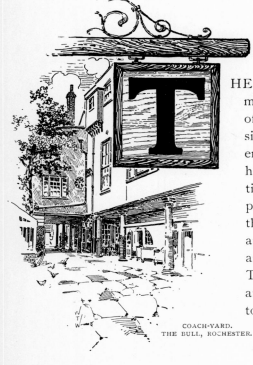

COACH-YARD.
THE BULL, ROCHESTER.

THE period we have now reached was marked by two special features—the joy of life at Gadshill, and the ominous signs of that physical breakdown which ended in an all-too-early death. Gadshill Place, the realised ideal of a lifetime, was acquired when prosperity and position were well assured, and when the large family of children had reached an age to give the greatest possible amount of interest and companionship. The boys were going into businesses and professions, the girls were old enough to take part in the hospitality of the house and in the endless activities of their father. The love for long walks received a fresh impetus from the old-new surroundings of natural beauty and historic interest. With parties of friends, with

COOLING CHURCH.

"Churchyard !" repeated my sister. "If it warn't for me you d have been to the churchyard long ago, and stayed there."—*Great Expectations.*

Miss Hogarth and some of the children, or sometimes with only a couple of great faithful dogs, Dickens took walks of tremendous length, and generally at a rapid rate, revisiting the scenes of Pickwick, and of his own boyhood and honeymoon days, and finding suggestions for *Great Expectations* and for *Edwin Drood*, which were yet to be written. A friend who accompanied many of those walks tells us how, at times, Dickens would seem to completely ignore his companions, striding ahead for miles, at a speed they could scarcely maintain, and answering their remarks only by absent-minded monosyllables. More often, throwing aside all cares and work, he showed the exuberant spirits of a boy, and was the very life of his party. At Gadshill Place itself there were many interests and occupations. Sinking a deep well ; boring a tunnel under the Dover Road to connect two parts of the property ; filling in a small lake, lest the younger children might be drowned ; erecting a sundial, made from a baluster of Rochester Bridge ; building and fitting a Swiss châlet sent over in sections by Fechter ; adding a conservatory to one end of the house ; and a host of similar activities, kept the busy versatile brain always at work. Everything was personally superintended, in every detail. The house itself was a model of order, cleanliness, and perfection of detail, and herein was seen the master's hand, for he went through every room, each morning.   His writing hours were strictly kept, and playing hours were just as religiously kept clear of work, thus showing a great change from the early days when he worked almost day and night. So great had the feeling of orderliness become that even the absence of certain ornaments, paper-weights, &c., from the desk was sufficient to interrupt the train of thought and make writing impossible.   On the other hand, some of Dickens's personal habits were irregular in the extreme. His long walks were begun at almost any hour of day or night (except working

FONT IN COOLING CHURCH.

"I pondered whether the church would be powerful enough to shield me from the vengeance of the terrible young man."
—*Great Expectations.*

time), and it is impossible to point to any room at Gadshill as Mr. Dickens's bedroom, for he often took a fancy to change from one room to another.

At holiday times athletic sports were organised for the villagers, and although thousands of rough men attended, and no police arrangements were made, the best possible order was kept and not an atom of damage was done.   Every detail of the children's education and all their personal interests were watched by the father; his letters to his boys were models of parental correspondence, and his pleasure and pride in them is constantly shown in his letters to friends, as in one to M. de Cerjat, in 1860, in which he tells how Charles is going to Hong Kong, where Frank is to join him later; Sydney is to enter the Navy; Walter is in India, another son at a French school, and the youngest at home.

Fragile from his childhood, Dickens had often broken down,

temporarily, under the enormous strain of his engagements, but in 1864 more serious symptoms became apparent, and developed as will be shown in the next chapter.

The principal events of this time must be very briefly summarised. The writing of *Great Expectations*, and its publication in *All the Year Round*, were decided upon at a staff council held in the office of that magazine on September 25th, 1860. *All the Year Round* had not had a Dickens serial running for some time, its sale was dropping slightly, and it was felt that an important work should be commenced at once. The first chapters were published on December 1st. In March and April, 1861, there was a series of readings in St. James's Hall, London; and in October a long series of provincial readings, continuing well into the next year, was begun. November and December of 1862 were spent in Paris, where readings were in demand, but "ten days were kept clear of readings" to give time for writing the Christmas number for the year; and in November, too, Charles Dickens, jun., married Miss Evans, daughter of the Mr. Evans who (in Bradbury and Evans) had so long been one of Dickens's printers and publishers. In January and February, 1863, Dickens was still in France and gave readings in Paris, and in March he began a series of Friday readings in London. In September, 1863, Mrs. John Dickens died; on December 24th, the sudden death of Thackeray came as a great shock; but a still greater was in store for Dickens's birthday, 1864, when he heard of the death of his son Walter, which had occurred in India on the last day of 1863.

In May, 1864, the publication of *Our Mutual Friend* began, and in the first three days the sale of the first number reached the thirtieth thousand. The publication was completed in November of 1865. Certain events of 1865 belong properly to the subject of the next chapter.

We have the authority of Mr. Henry F. Dickens for saying that his father regarded *Great Expectations* as the most perfect of his works, although he always had the greatest personal fondness for *David*

SOME SCENES FROM "GREAT EXPECTATIONS."

LITTLE BRITAIN.

TOWN HALL, ROCHESTER.

COVENT GARDEN.

TAVISTOCK HOTEL.

"SATIS HOUSE" FROM THE VINES.

THE "DICK WHITTINGTON."

ESSEX STREET.

O

Copperfield, in which so many of his youthful reminiscences were recorded. In "Pip," as in Copperfield, we may trace many reflections from the real life of the novelist, and there can be little doubt that the growth of Pip's character was based on memories of introspec-

COTTAGES (FORMERLY THE FORGE), COOLING.

"Joe's forge adjoined our house, which was a wooden house."—*Great Expectations*.

tion and self-exam-ination. Pip, as a study, emphasises a period between child-hood and manhood, which was less fully dealt with in Cop-perfield. The scenes of *Great Expecta-tions* are principally laid in the neighbour-hood of Gadshill, beginning with the churchyard of Cool-

ing, in which there is an actual original of the grave of "Philip Pirrip, late of this parish," with "five little stone lozenges" repre-senting the graves of Pip's young brethren; only that in the original the five lozenges are represented by a dozen, displayed on both sides of the principal stone. The Marshes, or "meshes," provide a most suitable atmosphere of gloom for the miserable convict's efforts to escape. The hamlet of Cooling has an inn, the "Horseshoe and Castle," prototype of the "Three Jolly Bargemen," and although there is now no blacksmith's forge, there is a cottage *called* the forge, which we are told was never used for that purpose, and a short row of cottages, which were in Dickens's time the forge and the black-smith's cottage, although nothing in their name or present appear-ance indicates the fact. Mr. Pumblechook's premises, in the High Street (Rochester) are supposed to have been the same as Mr. Sapsea's house (*Drood*), the quaint four-storied many-gabled place opposite the Nuns' House, which we shall see in the next chapter.

Miss Havisham's Satis House stands overlooking The Vines (now a public park). Its real name is Restoration House, and the name Dickens gave to it is taken from another house, on Boley Hill, not far away. The Town Hall, where Pip was apprenticed to Joe Gargery, stands in the High Street; and there is no objection to our passing through the open door and up the stairs to the justice room. The "Blue Boar" is none other than our old friend the "Bull Inn," and even the room where Mr. Wopsle "gave us Collins's ode" can

THE HORSESHOE AND CASTLE, COOLING.
"Joe had been at the Three Jolly Bargemen from a quarter after eight o'clock to a quarter before ten."—*Great Expectations.*

be identified by the fact that it was over the Commercial room. The "Cross Keys," Wood Street, where Pip, like the little boy Dickens, was deposited by the "Blue-Eyed Maid," exists no more, but Little Britain, Smithfield, Barnard's Inn, Gerrard Street (Soho), and the Dick Whittington, all connected with Pip's dealings with Mr. Jaggers, are still to be found. Garden Court, of the Temple, is so altered by the Thames Embankment that the reference to chambers "down by the river" has not the force it once had. The chambers themselves have been re-built, but behind them are the old houses in Essex Street, in one of which the convict, Magwitch, found shelter. The various gates of the Temple are mentioned; perhaps the most interesting is the Whitefriars Gate, where Pip received Wemmick's laconic warning, "Don't go Home." The Hummums in Covent Garden has been re-built, and the waterside districts are greatly altered, although there still remains much old-world flavour about "the Pool below Bridge" and the neighbourhood of Limehouse and Greenwich. To refresh his memory of these scenes, and to prepare details for the terribly realistic Chapter LIV, dealing with the attempt to get Magwitch out of the country, Dickens chartered a steamer from Blackwall to Southend, on May 22nd, 1861, and made it the occasion of a picnic, of which Forster says :—"Eight or nine friends and three or four members of his family were on board, and he seemed to have no care, the whole of that summer day, except to enjoy their enjoyment and entertain them with his own in shape of a thousand whims and fancies ; but his sleepless observation was at work all the time, and nothing had escaped his keen vision on either

WHITEFRIARS GATE, THE TEMPLE.
"It seldom happened that I came in at that Whitefriars Gate after the Temple was closed."—*Great Expectations*.

side of the river. The fifteenth chapter of the third volume is a masterpiece." Beside those we have mentioned, a few other localities occur, but the one of most importance, Wemmick's "Castle" at Walworth, can never be identified, and we must be content to picture it in imagination, from Dickens's humorous description.

Our Mutual Friend, so intimately connected with the Thames, gives a multitude of generalised, rather than particularised scenes. It gives, most wonderfully, the flavour of that damp, muddy, water-side life, which Dickens had first known in the days of Hungerford Stairs, and which, partly by the attraction of repulsion, and partly by its varied picturesqueness, always fascinated him. The work of Rogue Riderhood, between and about the bridges of Southwark and London, and the scenes at the "Six Jolly Fellowship Porters," show intimate knowledge of a somewhat seamy side of life, gained in association with the river police, a body of men whom Dickens greatly admired.

THE SWISS CHÂLET.
Given to Dickens by Fechter.   Now in Cobham Park.

Boffin's Bower, or Harmony Jail, the home of the Golden Dustman, was on the spot now occupied by the Great Northern Railway, close to York Road Station, and the golden dust-heaps had an actual existence in Dickens's boyish days, when they came into the view as he looked across from Bayham Street to the City and St. Paul's. More than one "corner house not far from Cavendish Square" would still provide a stand for Silas Wegg; and the actual original of Mr. Venus's shop may be seen at No. 42, Great St. Andrew Street, Seven Dials, although Dickens locates it in Clerkenwell. The place and the peculiar trade of the anatomist were discovered for the author by his illustrator, Mr. Marcus Stone. The "dismal churchyard" on the north of the Temple

INTERIOR (UPPER ROOM) OF CHÂLET.
Where Dickens wrote his last works.

Church is no longer dismal, but from it we may see the same window which Dickens imagined as that of Mortimer Lightwood's office ; and not far away is Clifford's Inn, where Mr. Boffin engaged Rokesmith as his secretary. Sackville Street, Piccadilly; Duke Street, St. James's; St. James's Church; Portman Square; the Albany; Westminster Hall; "the garden up by the Trinity House on Tower Hill";

SOME "MUTUAL FRIEND" SCENES.

| THE ALBANY. | ST. JOHN'S, WESTMINSTER. | THE RED LION, HENLEY. |
| ORIGINAL OF MR. VENUS'S. | CLIFFORD'S INN. | SMITH SQUARE. |

Limehouse Church; Mincing Lane; the church, park, and observatory at Greenwich; and several places of minor interest, can easily be found by anyone who knows his London. The honeymoon of Mr. and Mrs. Lammle at Shanklin, Isle of Wight, was reminiscent of Dickens's own visits to the island; and he took the trouble to specially examine St. Mary Axe, to find a building suitable for Pubsey and Co., in which he could place the kindly Mr. Riah, a character purposely drawn to offset that of Fagin, in justice to the Jews. The house no longer stands. Millbank and the Vauxhall Bridge district are passed beyond recognition in the march of improvements, but Church Street still leads into Smith Square, and "where the street and square joined" are still "some little quiet houses in a row," reminding us of Jenny Wren and her "bad boy." The Ship Tavern, in Greenwich, is where the "lovely woman" and her father

WAPPING OLD STAIRS.

A typical bit of the waterside district of *Great Expectations* and *Our Mutual Friend*.

dined at the time of their "elopement," and where the marriage dinner was held after the wedding of that same lady to John Rokesmith.

The up-river scenes include Hampton, where Mortimer Lightwood and Eugene Wrayburn had a bachelor cottage; Brentford, where poor Betty Higden tended her interesting "minder"; and the places mentioned in connection with Betty's pilgrimage, through Chertsey, Walton, Kingston, and Staines. Hurley Lock is supposed to have been the original of Plashwater Mill Weir Lock. Rogue Riderhood described its distance as "twenty mile and odd—call it five-and-twenty mile and odd if you like," and Hurley Lock is about twenty-five miles in a straight line, although it is nearly fifty by river. The Paper Mill, where Lizzie Hexam found work, and near which Betty Higden died, was no doubt Marsh Mill, a mile or so above Henley; in which case the tow-path below Henley was the scene of Headstone's attempt to murder Wrayburn, and the " Red Lion " was the inn where Wrayburn was nursed after his rescue by Lizzie Hexam, and where they were married.

THE TOWER OF LONDON.

Which dominates the waterside district of *Great Expectations* and *Our Mutual Friend*.

"THE MONK'S VINEYARD" (THE VINES), ROCHESTER.

"Among the elm trees by the Cathedral, they stopped as by consent, and Rosa raised her face to his, as she had never raised it in the old days."—*Edwin Drood*.

CHAPTER XII

The Second American Tour, "Edwin Drood," Final Readings, the Close of Life

1865–1870

THE DICK WHITTINGTON, CLOTHFAIR, LONDON.

RUSKIN, writing a few years after Dickens's death, said: "The miserable death of poor Dickens, when he might have been writing blessed books till he was eighty, but for the pestiferous demands of the mob, is a very solemn warning to all of us," and in these words expressed the idea, doubtless a correct one, that Dickens was killed by the strain of his public readings. These enormous efforts, both in Britain and America, absorbed almost the whole of the novelist's time and power during

DICKENS'S SUN-DIAL: FROM
GADSHILL.

the last few years of his life, so that the history of this period must deal with the reading, rather than the writing of books.

Constantly on the verge of physical and nervous break-down, even from his early years, Dickens had made his life a series of splendid efforts, with frequent short snatches of enforced rest between, and although the warning illnesses became more frequent and more dangerous in later life, he was spurred on by his restless energy and tempted to rely too much upon his enormous and oft-tried power of recuperation. From almost the earliest books Dickens had been in the habit of reading his manuscripts to a small circle of friends. From this to the semi-public reading of part of Dombey, at Lausanne in 1846, was a very natural step, giving rise to the suggestion that "a great deal of money might possibly be made (if it were not *infra dig.*) by one's having readings of one's own books." The idea was opposed by Forster, but later came readings for charity, and gradually the temptation of the enormous profits to be made by reading for a comparatively small number of times overcame all opposition. In all (excluding those undertaken for charity), Dickens gave over four hundred public readings, which earned him some £45,000; a magnificent result if health and life had not been sacrificed.

A serious physical warning was received in February, 1865, when great pain and lameness

TUNNEL UNDER DOVER ROAD.
Driven by Dickens to connect his two gardens

of the left foot checked the long walks which had hitherto been as safety-valves for restless energy. Attributing the trouble to frost-bite, and regarding it as purely local, Dickens missed the real importance of the attack; and he also disregarded a slight

GADSHILL PLACE.
Dickens's library to right of porch.

sun-stroke and frequent return of his old catarrhal trouble. To aggravate these difficulties, and as a great shock to the already over-strained nerves, came a terrible railway accident on June 9th, 1865, at Staplehurst. Many lives were lost; Dickens was preserved unhurt, as if by a miracle, and although he worked with complete coolness and great strength for hours amongst the dead and dying, the shock told upon him, very perceptibly, for a long time. It is doubtful if he ever completely regained his nerve, a fact which added greatly to the strain of the travel between the readings, and which shows how strong must have been the will that arranged and carried out long series of readings in all parts of Great Britain and Ireland, and in America. Early in 1866, Dickens was examined by two doctors, who reported disease of the heart, but in spite of that, he made an agreement with Messrs. Chappell & Sons to give thirty readings, wherever they chose, in England, Scotland, Ireland, or Paris, Messrs. Chappell paying every expense, including personal

GADSHILL AND DISTRICT.

OLD HIGHAM CHURCH.   REAR OF GADSHILL PLACE.
DOVER ROAD, WITH CEDARS AT GADSHILL.   SITE OF THE CHÂLET.

and travelling charges of the reader and his staff, in addition to a clear fee of £50 per night. George Dolby was the manager of the tour, and Dickens had every reason to be grateful to the Chappells, to Dolby, and to his travelling servants, for easing his work to an enormous extent.

In the earliest readings, the Trial scene from *Pickwick*, Bob Sawyer's tea party, from the same book, and the scenes at Squeers's School, from *Nicholas Nickleby*, provided the more mirthful portion, while Boots at the Holly Tree Inn gave a tone of quaint quiet humour, and a selection from *Dr. Marigold's Prescriptions* provided that pathos which moved whole audiences to tears. The readings were enormously popular. At Liverpool, for instance, the police reported that three thousand people tried and failed to obtain admission at the doors.

SCENES OF "SEVEN POOR TRAVELLERS."

| WASHING PLACE. | REAR OF WATTS'S CHARITY. | WATTS'S CHARITY. |
| KITCHEN OF BULL INN. | DORMITORY LANDING. | SUPPER ROOM. |

At other places the people were so insistent that, in addition to filling every place where it was possible to sit or stand, they crowded and lay down upon the very platform itself. This enormous crowding added to Dickens's responsibility and anxiety, but he was always able to hold every member of his audience, and in the few cases when accidents to the lights threatened panic amongst the more nervous auditors, he kept them in their places by sheer personal influence. Well might the gas-man say, "The master is *grand.*"

At the close of the first series of readings under the Chappells management, Dickens suggested a further engagement for forty-two nights for £2,500, or £60 a night, "and every conceivable and inconceivable expense paid"; and this was at once accepted for readings in the winter of 1866. For the spring of 1867 he planned and carried out a series of fifty more readings. Invitations from America became more and more pressing, and on the 3rd of August, 1867, Dickens sent Dolby to the States to personally inspect the field and consider the prospects. The report was favourable, and at the end of September, after a consultation with Dolby and Forster, "Yes!" was telegraphed to Boston. On November 2nd, a farewell banquet was given to the novelist in the Freemasons' Hall, Lord Lytton presiding, and on November 9th Dickens sailed for Boston.

RICHARD WATTS'S MONUMENT, AND TABLET TO DICKENS.
ROCHESTER CATHEDRAL.

"The effigy of Master Richard Watts was bursting out of his
tomb."—*Seven Poor Travellers.*

If the success in Britain had been great, that in the United States was simply phenomenal. The most extravagant speculation in tickets at enormous premiums occurred, in spite of every effort of Dickens and his manager to sell to bona-fide buyers. The speculators hired gangs of men to form in line at the ticket-offices, and eventually they were obliged to be on the ground so early that many of them brought mattresses and camped for the night, while a profitable trade was carried on in supplying them with refreshments.   Return visits to the principal cities found the enthusiasm greater, rather than less,

EASTGATE HOUSE (THE " NUNS' HOUSE "), ROCHESTER.
" In the midst of Cloisterham stands the Nuns' House ; a venerable brick edifice."—*Edwin Drood.*

and through all the series of readings there was no evidence that the work could not be carried on indefinitely.   But the fatigue was awful !   Inclement weather, long journeys, including some in which the trains crawled for hours through flood-water and ice that reached the axles, constant catarrh, relaxed throat and loss of voice, and constant pain in the left foot, with frequent and alarming heart troubles, made a combination of ills against which only the most invincible will-power could successfully struggle.   There were one or two cases in which reading was absolutely impossible, and the engagement had to be postponed under doctors' imperative orders, but in most cases, even when the reader seemed quite collapsed and unable to articulate immediately before the opening time, the feeling of the platform and sight of the audience brought back voice and power, and he went through his programme amidst breathless attention, with

A ROOM IN THE "NUNS' HOUSE."

"Mr. Grewgious was discovered by his ward, much discomfited by being in Miss Twinkleton's company, in Miss Twinkleton's own sacred room."—*Edwin Drood*.

occasional bursts of rapturous applause, only to drop in complete exhaustion the moment he left the platform.

In spite of the labour of reading, and the strain of travel, Dickens found time for many social and other engagements, such as a dinner with Longfellow, Emerson, Wendell Holmes, and Agassiz; and negotiations for the production of a stage version of *No Thoroughfare*. He even found relaxation in arranging a walking-match, in Boston, between George Dolby and J. R. Osgood, both of whom had been travelling with him, for which he drew up a humorous and most elaborate series of "Articles of Agreement." A brilliant day at Niagara, which was made a holiday for the benefit of the staff, made an enjoyable little break in the labours. On April 18th, 1868, Dickens was guest of honour at a dinner by the New York Press

ROCHESTER SCENES OF "EDWIN DROOD."

THE CATHEDRAL CRYPT.	"MR. TOPE."	THE CATHEDRAL.
"MR. SAPSEA'S HOUSE."	MINOR CANON CORNER.	"JASPER'S GATEHOUSE."

Club, on the 20th his last American reading was given, and on the 22nd the party sailed for home by the *Russia*.

Late in the same year Dickens declined the request that he should become a Member of Parliament for Edinburgh, and early in October he began a long final series of readings. In April of 1869, the gravity of his illness compelled the summoning of a physician, who insisted on the readings being immediately abandoned for a year. The provincial engagements were cancelled, but Dickens's feeling of responsibility to Messrs. Chappell made him undertake a series of Farewell Readings, in St. James's Hall, London, commencing

P

January 11th, 1870, and concluding with an enormously successful reading and farewell speech on March 15th.

The readings were done just as earnestly and thoroughly as any other part of Dickens's work. After the very first they were not truly "readings" at all, for they were learned by heart, and constantly rehearsed, even when in regular reading before the public. In addition to the subjects already mentioned, the death of Paul Dombey, and *A Christmas Carol*, were wonderfully popular ; and for the latest readings Dickens got up the terribly powerful scene of the murder of Nancy by Bill Sikes, from *Oliver Twist*. When first given in public, as Nancy fell back with a dying shriek, the effect was so electrical that a large number of ladies fainted and had to be carried from the hall. This climax was dropped in the remaining presentations, but the murder scene took such a hold on Dickens that it always left him completely wrecked. Yet "in justice to his managers" he refused to drop such a powerful item. Audiences were completely dominated by the readings, and the effect may be summed up in the comment of Carlyle, who, when some one remarked that Dickens was a born actor, retorted—"Actor ! why, the man's a whole theatre."

The constant whirl of reading and travel prevented much attention to writing, but in August, 1869, *Edwin Drood* was outlined, and on the 26th of October, the manuscript of the first number was read at Forster's house to a small party. Dickens was absorbed by the story, and probably had never written better. The plot interested and satisfied him, and the principal scenes were laid in Rochester, which he touched and described lovingly and delicately as "Cloisterham." Most of the places can be easily recognised. The Cathedral, the Close, the esplanade below the Castle walls, the Monks' Vineyard (locally called The Vines), Minor Canon Corner (really Minor Canon Row), the Nuns' House (Eastgate House, now a public museum), and Mr. Sapsea's house, just across the High Street from Eastgate House. Jasper's Gatehouse is usually identified with the College Gatehouse in High Street, but there are details in Dickens's description which fit each of the three gates of the Close, while no one of them answers in all points. The Travellers' Twopenny, in Gasworks Garden, cannot be identified, and the opium den of Lascar Sal, in London (which was described from an actual original) has been destroyed. Staple

STAPLE INN, LONDON.

INNER COURT, THE HALL.   INNER COURT, MR. GREWGIOUS'S ROOMS.
                    HOLBORN FRONTAGE.
OUTER COURT.   OUTER COURT.

Inn, Holborn, still remains, in part. We may see dear old Mr. Grewgious's rooms, and even the mark J P T over the entrance; we 1747 may see the window from which peered the evil face of John Jasper, but the part of the Inn where Neville Landless lodged has been swept away; as has the neighbouring Inn, where Mr. Grewgious secured for Rosa Bud "the prettiest chamber in Furnival's." Cloisterham Weir has no original in the Rochester district. Probably it was imported from the Upper Thames by the writer's imagination. We

P 2

cannot be quite sure of the course taken by Neville Landless on the morning after Drood's disappearance, but we imagine it was along

THE GRAVEYARD IN THE MOAT OF ROCHESTER CASTLE.
Where Dickens wished to be buried.

the road over Blue Bell hill to Maidstone, where a suitable place can be found for his turning into the by-lane and his arrest.

Edwin Drood was proceeding smoothly and fluently, for Dickens felt the relief from strain and the pleasure of return to familiar work. He wrote in the upper room of the châlet given by Fechter, which he had placed amongst the grand cedar trees of his garden, lined with mirrors, so that the sunshine and the birds and the leaves might be reflected and re-reflected.

On a brilliant summer day, the 8th of June, he was so much interested in the story that, contrary to custom, he resumed work after lunch, and continued writing through the afternoon. At dinner, Miss Hogarth remarked a look of pain and trouble, and was told

DICKENS'S GRAVE, WESTMINSTER ABBEY.

With plain inscription, name and dates, as provided in his will.

that he had been very ill for an hour. Shortly afterward he attempted to rise, staggered, and was helped to the ground, where he lay unconscious until death on the evening of June 9th, the fifth anniversary of the Staplehurst accident.

Dickens had wished that his remains should be laid in the little graveyard in the moat of Rochester Castle, but this had been closed for interments ; the family proposed to bury him in the Church-yard of Shorne, but the nation claimed his honoured remains for Westminster Abbey.

Of the many tributes to the great writer's memory none was more spontaneous or touching than that by the late Mr. Bret Harte, in the *Overland Monthly*, under the title of "Dickens in Camp." The mourning and the tributes were universal, for the whole world felt the loss of a leader and a friend, and some one drew attention to the fact that amongst the last words written before the pen dropped from Dickens's hand for ever, were these :—

"Changes of glorious light from moving boughs, songs of birds, scents from gardens, woods, and fields—or, rather, from the one great garden of the whole cultivated island in its yielding time—penetrate into the Cathedral, subdue its earthy odour, and preach the Resurrection and the Life. The cold stone tombs of centuries ago grow warm ; and flecks of brightness dart into the sternest marble corners of the building, fluttering there like wings."

THE END

ROCKINGHAM (CHESNEY WOLD) VILLAGE.

END OF MY LADY'S WALK

ROCKINGHAM: WITH MR. TULKINGHORN'S TOWER.

SOME "BLEAK HOUSE" SCENES.

INDEX
And partial directory to the Land of Charles Dickens

THE impossibility of even mentioning any adequate part of the places named in the works of Charles Dickens in the body of our book, induces us to combine with the Index a general list of places. This is not exhaustive, either as regards the places mentioned or the writings in which they occur, but it will enable the reader to find a greater number of scenes than has been identified in any previous book on Dickens's topography—perhaps more than all such books combined.

This form of index seems, on the whole, more useful than a series of maps. The London scenes may best be found by using one of the pocket atlases with index, such as John Walker's, Bacon's, Bartholomew's, etc.

The following abbreviations, used after names of places or persons, indicate the works in which reference is made to them, viz. :

B=**B**leak House	**I**=Pictures from **I**taly	**R**=Barnaby **R**udge
C=**C**opperfield	**L**=**L**ittle Dorrit	**Rep**=**Rep**rinted Pieces
D=**D**ombey and Son	**M**=**M**artin Chuzzlewit	**S**=**S**ketches by Boz
E=**E**dwin Drood	**Mast. H**=**Mast**er **H**umphrey's Clock	**Sil**=George **Sil**verman's Explanation
F=Our Mutual Friend	**N**=**N**icholas Nickleby	**T**=**T**ale of Two Cities
G=**G**reat Expectations	**O**=**O**liver Twist	**U**=**U**ncommercial Traveller
H=**H**ard Times	**P**=**P**ickwick	**X**=**X**mas Stories and Books
Hunt=**Hunt**ed Down	**Q**=Old Cu(**Q**)riosity Shop	

An asterisk [*] indicates an illustration.
Italics used for the names of persons or places indicate that they are fictitious names given by Dickens.
Suggestions as to omissions which may seem serious will be heartily welcomed.

VIEWS OF WARMINGTON,
NEAR BANBURY.

THE VILLAGE WHERE
LITTLE NELL MET THE
SCHOOLMASTER.

R. CLAY AND SONS, LTD., BREAD ST. HILL, E.C., AND BUNGAY, SUFFOLK.